CAMBRIDGE copy COLLECTION

In Business

Activities to bring Business English to life

Marjorie Rosenberg

CAMBRIDGE
UNIVERSITY PRESS

CAMBRIDGE UNIVERSITY PRESS
Cambridge, New York, Melbourne, Madrid, Cape Town, Singapore, São Paulo

Cambridge University Press
The Edinburgh Building, Cambridge CB2 2RU, UK

www.cambridge.org
Information on this title: www.cambridge.org/9780521617291

First published 2005

Printed in the United Kingdom at the University Press, Cambridge

Design and page makeup by Kamae design.

A catalogue record for this book is available from the British Library

ISBN -13 978-0-521-61729-1
ISBN -10 0-521-61729-4

Acknowledgements

I would like to thank Clare Abbott from Cambridge University Press for all the advice and help she has given me in creating *In Business*. In addition, I would like to thank Sally Searby for believing in this project and helping make it possible. I am also very grateful to Tony Garside for his insights, patience and general brilliance in editing this book.

A big thank you also goes to my colleagues Elke Beder for help with the negotiations and email exercises and Marie-Lou Schönbacher-Cuyt, who gave me feedback on a number of the activities as well as providing me with the original idea for the marketing concept game. A business English book also needs professional support and here I am grateful to Franz Kerber, member of the board at the Steiermärkische Bank und Sparkassen AG in Graz, Austria who worked through the activities dealing with finances and balance sheets and Karen Glass, Assistant Sales Manager of Blair Television, New York City who helped out with the sales activity. Their input was invaluable.

I would also like to mention my English students at both the Pädagogische Akademie des Bundes in Graz and the Berufspädagogische Akademie in Graz as well as the participants in the Teaching Business English at Nile in Norwich, England. They willingly did many of the activities and provided ideas and feedback.

Last but not least, I would like to thank my partner, Michael Hanacek, of Chrysler, Austria, whose cutting edge knowledge of technology and international business English is enormously helpful. I can't imagine writing a book without his help.

Map of the book

Introduction page 7

Activity	Page	Type	Time	Level	Language focus	Grouping	One-to-one
1 At work							
1.1 Pay and benefits	9	Matching + gap-fill	20 minutes	Intermediate / B1	Collocations	Pairs or small groups	Yes
1.2 Pay and benefits crossword	13	Information gap	20–30 minutes	Intermediate / B1	Defining terms	Whole class in two groups	Yes
1.3 Jobs and descriptions	16	Matching	20–30 minutes	Intermediate / B1	Jobs and job descriptions	Whole class	Yes
2 Organizations							
2.1 Words and definitions	18	Matching	20 minutes	Upper intermediate–Advanced / B2–C1	Defining terms	Individual or pairs	Yes
2.2 Characteristics of organizations	20	Categorizing	15–20 minutes	Upper intermediate–Advanced / B2–C1	Types of organization	Pairs or small groups	Yes
2.3 Cooperative crossword	23	Information gap	20–30 minutes	Upper intermediate–Advanced / B2–C1	Organizations and how they are set up	Groups of four	Yes
3 Telephoning							
3.1 Phone dialogues	27	Sorting and ordering	20 minutes	Intermediate–Upper intermediate / B1–B2	Telephoning language	Pairs or small groups	Yes
3.2 Phone phrases	30	Four in a row (noughts and crosses) game	20–30 minutes	Intermediate–Upper intermediate / B1–B2	Telephoning language	Pairs	Yes
4 Emails							
4.1 Addresses	33	Exchanging information	10–20 minutes	Pre-intermediate / B1	The alphabet and symbols /punctuation used in email addresses	Whole class	Yes
4.2 Email styles	35	Sorting and ordering	15 minutes	Pre-intermediate–Intermediate / B1	Formal and informal phrases for emails	Pairs or small groups	Yes
4.3 Making an arrangement	37	Matching and ordering	15 minutes	Pre-intermediate–Intermediate / B1	Functions and formal and informal phrases for emails	Individual or pairs	Yes

Activity	Page	Type	Time	Level	Language focus	Grouping	One-to-one
5 Buying and selling							
5.1 Hard and soft sell	40	Ordering	20 minutes	Upper intermediate–Advanced / B2–C1	Sales pitches	Pairs or small groups	Yes
5.2 The marketplace	42	Role play	30–40 minutes	Upper intermediate–Advanced / B2–C1	Language for buying and selling products	Whole class	Yes
6 Marketing							
6.1 The marketing mix	45	Ordering	20–30 minutes	Upper intermediate–Advanced / B2–C1	Marketing mix terms	Pairs or small groups	Yes
6.2 A marketing strategy	48	Creating a marketing strategy	30–45 minutes	Upper intermediate–Advanced / B2–C1	Marketing terms	Small groups	Yes
6.3 Advertising	50	Ordering Creating an advertisement	30–45 minutes	Upper intermediate–Advanced / B2–C1	Language to describe products; language of persuasion	Pairs or small groups	Yes
7 Finance							
7.1 Terms used in balance sheets	53	Matching	30 minutes	Intermediate–Upper intermediate / B1–B2	Balance sheet terms	Groups of three	Yes
7.2 The balance sheet	57	Information gap	15 minutes	Intermediate–Upper intermediate / B1–B2	Balance sheet terms; numbers	Pairs	Yes
7.3 Financial news	61	Correct the mistakes	20–30 minutes	Intermediate–Upper intermediate / B1–B2	Balance sheets and financial reports; language of change	Pairs	Yes
7.4 Finance triangle	63	Matching	15 minutes	Intermediate–Upper intermediate / B1–B2	Terms used in balance sheets and financial reports	Groups of three	Yes
8 Marketing and finance terms							
8.1 Find someone who knows …	65	Find someone who …	10–15 minutes	Intermediate / B1	Common business terms for marketing and finance	Whole class	Yes
8.2 Definitions	67	Defining terms + matching	20 minutes	Intermediate / B1	Common business terms for marketing and finance	Pairs or small groups	Yes

Activity	Page	Type	Time	Level	Language focus	Grouping	One-to-one
9 The meeting							
The new canteen	70	Holding a meeting	60 minutes+	Upper intermediate–Advanced / B2–C1	Language of meetings, e.g. asking for and giving opinions	Groups of four to six	Not suitable
10 Negotiations							
10.1 Dealing with colleagues	73	Matching	10–15 minutes	Intermediate / B1	Language of bargaining and reaching agreement	Pairs	Yes
10.2 Departmental heads	75	Role play	45–60 minutes	Upper intermediate–Advanced / B2–C1	Language of negotiations	Groups of four	Yes
11 Presentations							
11.1 Key phrases	78	Gap-fill	20 minutes	Intermediate–Upper intermediate / B1–B2	Presentations phrases	Pairs or small groups	Yes
11.2 Giving a presentation	82	Presenting and giving feedback	30–40 minutes +	Upper intermediate–Advanced / B2–C1	Language of presentations; linking words	Whole class	Yes
12 Cross-cultural awareness							
The culture game	86	Board game	20–30 minutes	Intermediate–Upper intermediate / B1–B2	Vocabulary related to customs and cultures	Groups of three to five	Yes
13 British and American English							
13.1 UK or US?	89	Information gap	20 minutes	Intermediate / B1	British vs American terms	Groups of four	Yes
13.2 British/American triangle	95	Matching	15 minutes	Intermediate / B1	British vs American terms	Groups of three	Yes

Introduction

Methodology

Learners of Business English were long treated as more 'serious' learners than those attending general English classes. This might have to do with the fact that they were sent to classes to improve their current job possibilities or to expand into new fields. In any case, the job of the Business English trainer was to make sure that they left the classroom armed with the specialized vocabulary and language competence they needed to succeed in the workplace.

As we continue to explore how learners actually learn best, we have found that learners of Business English are also eager to enjoy their lessons. We have found that enjoyment of lessons actually raises motivation and produces longer retention of the material, leading to more effective learning. Therefore, the last several years have seen a number of photocopiable materials designed to help both teachers and learners discover the 'fun' element in learning Business English.

In Business has been created with this element of fun and self-discovery in mind. It contains student-centred supplementary material designed to accompany any business course, with activities for different levels and types of learners. The topics cover several of the basic areas which learners meet in their business studies classes and give learners the opportunity to review what they have learned in an alternative way. This can reinforce the learning effect and help learners to understand more completely the material they have dealt with elsewhere.

The assumption is that most learners will enjoy games and activities that help them to learn. In this book, the various learning styles that individuals have are catered for, and there are activities to suit all types:

Visual (need to see the material) – matching games, jigsaw reading, crossword puzzles, writing activities

Auditory (need to speak and listen) – pair and group activities, with discussions included or suggested as part of the feedback

Kinaesthetic (need to touch things and move about) – cards to manipulate, opportunities to walk around the classroom, group work and a board game

Analytic (like details and systematic learning) – problems to solve and situations to analyse

Global (prefer to see an overview and value group work) – co-operative activities and the opportunity to exchange ideas with other learners

The activities

The activities comprising *In Business* cover a number of different areas, from everyday office situations such as email and telephoning, through key business functions like presenting and negotiating, to topics such as buying and selling, which allow for discussion as well as practical language acquisition. Each activity has accompanying notes to guide the teacher through the activity and to provide suggestions and key vocabulary where appropriate.

Flexibility

One of the main considerations in the development of this material has been the need for teachers and learners to adapt to different situations, and flexibility has been built in in a number of ways. In each topic area there is usually more than one activity. This allows for an element of progression in the activities meaning it is possible to work through from the first activity to the last, practising and learning more about the topic with each activity. However, it is not necessary to do one before going on to the next, and each can be seen as an independent, stand-alone activity. Depending in part on the level of the learners and the time available, the teacher may prefer to omit, for example, Activity 1.1 and go straight into Activity 1.2. The lead-in section of the Teacher's notes will help the teacher to cover whatever is needed to do any given activity without having to do the preceding one.

The Teacher's notes give information about timing, language level and group formation, all of which should be seen as a guide only, and teachers are encouraged to alter things to suit their needs. With regard to level, for example, an activity that is most appropriate for an intermediate class could be very useful quick revision for an advanced class.

Although many of the activities are designed to be done in classes where learners can move about, for example to find cards matching the ones they hold, it is also possible to give each group a set of cards and have them work together without moving around.

In groups which enjoy a more competitive atmosphere, many of the activities can be scored afterwards, with points awarded to groups or individuals who finish first and have the highest number of correct answers. In other situations, where co-operation is more highly valued, groups can mingle to help one another.

Feedback is important in these activities, as the learners need to discover the correct answers to the activities, and again, this can be approached in a number of ways: the teacher can go through the answers orally with the whole class, using the key or the original sheet which was copied and cut up as the cards are in the correct order there. This sheet, or the sheet with a separate key if there is one, can be photocopied and handed out to each learner to check their answers, or to one learner in a pair or group to check the answers for the others, or shown to the whole class on an OHP. Alternatively, pairs can give their feedback to the class before the teacher leads the discussion, or the pairs can check each other's answers before general class discussion. Learners can also be encouraged to look up words in dictionaries and discuss meanings with their partners or groups before asking the teacher for the correct answer.

Virtually all of the activities can be used in one-to-one teaching situations, with little or no adaptation, as explained in the Teacher's notes for each activity. Activities with worksheets can be used as they are, while activities involving cards can be done by the learner on his or her own or with the teacher being the other half of a 'pair'. Many learners in this type of teaching situation eagerly welcome the chance to do a kinaesthetic activity to break up the routine of just speaking with a teacher for the whole lesson. It is always a good idea to ask the learner how he or she prefers to learn and to adapt the material to his or her individual needs.

As one of the skills of teaching involves knowing what is best to do in specific situations, teachers can decide for themselves when to use which approach and vary it accordingly.

Photocopying

Modern photocopiers can generally be fed with paper which is heavier than the average, meaning that cards and board games can be copied directly onto thicker paper and used over and over again. When copying sets of cards for groups, it is best to use different coloured paper for each set of the same cards as this makes it much simpler to put the cards together at the end of the activity. If it is possible to laminate the cards, this ensures that they are usable for many classes.

Practical applications

The activities and the methods in *In Business* have been tried out in a number of different teaching situations and classes, ranging from Business English classes in language schools and in-company classes, to teacher training courses. The content of the topic areas has been chosen to cover a wide range of different areas of business, and the various ways in which the material is presented provide the flexibility to use *In Business* in a variety of contexts and situations, to promote not only learning but also enjoyment.

Pay and benefits

Type of activity
Matching + gap-fill

Time
20 minutes

Level
Intermediate / B1

Language focus
Common collocations dealing with pay and benefits

Group formation
Pairs or small groups

Preparation
Copy and cut up the dominoes, one set for each group.

Copy the sheet with sentences, one for each learner.

Lead-in
Brainstorm types of payment and benefits available to employees.

Elicit collocations such as *dental plan, minimum wage, fringe benefits* (or other collocations from the sentences that you feel might be difficult for your learners).

Procedure
- Divide the class into pairs or small groups and give out the dominoes.
- Explain how the game of dominoes is played: when the first domino has been put down, players must look for the domino which joins on to it, i.e. having a word on the left which goes with the word on the right on the domino that has been put down.
- Give out the sheet with the sentences and explain that each of the gaps will be filled by a two-word phrase which can be found when all the dominoes have been laid out in order.
- Instruct the learners to find the domino marked with an asterisk (*) next to the word on the right. Explain that the word on the right (*redundancy*) is the first part of the phrase which goes into the first gap in sentence number 1. Then tell them to look for a word on the left side of one of the dominoes which completes the phrase (*package*).
- When the learners have found this, tell them to complete the sentence and then read it to check the meaning.
- Explain that the first word fitting into the gaps in the second sentence is found on the right side of this second domino and tell the learners to continue working in this way, laying the dominoes out so that they are in the correct order corresponding with the sentences.
- When the learners have completed the exercise correctly, the last word completing sentence number 18 is the word to the left of *redundancy* (*sharing*).
- Discuss the answers with the learners (see Introduction).

Follow-up
Discuss benefits which participants receive, in small groups or with the whole class. Groups could also prioritize the benefits and discuss which ones are most important to them. The participants can decide among themselves which benefits they could more easily give up and which ones might influence their choice of a company to work for. If the learners are in management, the discussion could include management's view of the benefits offered to employees.

One-to-one
The teacher gives the sentences and dominoes to the learner. They discuss the results. The discussion can also include a prioritizing of benefits.

Vocabulary
cash bonus extra money paid to employees when they have done an exceptional job or the company has performed well
expense account money which a business person is allowed to spend on meals, travel, hotels, entertaining clients, etc.
flexible hours working hours which allow employees to choose when to start and finish work
fringe benefits extras given to an employee in addition to pay, such as a company car or health insurance
maternity leave time off from work after a woman has had a baby (often with pay, sometimes only with job guarantee)
perk an extra benefit for employees, such as free equipment, use of a company car or flat, etc.
redundancy package money paid to employees when they lose their jobs
spouse husband or wife
stock options the opportunity to buy company shares at below market price or to receive shares instead of cash bonuses
subsidized partially paid for by a company or government, e.g. a staff canteen

Gapped sentences

1 When people lose their jobs, they often get a ________ ________.

2 Some companies offer ________ ________ in addition to or instead of cash bonuses.

3 The lowest legal amount of money which can be paid to workers is called the ________ ________.

4 Managers often receive ________ ________ when their departments reach specific goals.

5 Some companies have a ________ ________ for their employees so that they can buy lunch at a reasonable price.

6 A company car and health insurance can be part of the ________ ________ of a job.

7 Most companies pay into a ________ ________ so their employees can have an income when they retire.

8 Some job advertisements give the ________ ________, and some give the hourly or monthly one.

9 Part of the health insurance package includes a ________ ________ so that people can take care of their teeth.

10 Women who have a baby can get time off, called ________ ________.

11 ________ ________ are offered by companies for people with small children.

12 An extra benefit is often offered as a form of ________ ________, which helps a spouse or family in the case of death of the wage earner.

13 People working in retail businesses get ________ ________ as part of their benefit packages.

14 A common perk for senior management is a ________ ________.

15 People in companies who often have to entertain clients usually have an ________ ________.

16 When employees fall ill, they can receive ________ ________ until they can return to work.

17 When employees work ________ ________, they have a certain amount of freedom to decide when they want to start and finish work.

18 Companies have found that ________ ________ is a way to deal with part-time workers.

Dominoes

sharing	redundancy *	package	stock
options	minimum	wage	performance-related
benefits	subsidized	canteen	fringe
benefits	pension	scheme	annual
salary	dental	plan	maternity
leave	childcare	facilities	life
insurance	employee	discounts	company
car	expense	account	sick
pay	flexible	hours	job

Key

1. When people lose their jobs, they often get a **redundancy package**.
2. Some companies offer **stock options** in addition to or instead of cash bonuses.
3. The lowest legal amount of money which can be paid to workers is called the **minimum wage**.
4. Managers often receive **performance-related benefits** when their departments reach specific goals.
5. Some companies have a **subsidized canteen** for their employees so that they can buy lunch at a reasonable price.
6. A company car and health insurance can be part of the **fringe benefits** of a job.
7. Most companies pay into a **pension scheme** so their employees can have an income when they retire.
8. Some job advertisements give the **annual salary**, and some give the hourly or monthly one.
9. Part of the health insurance package includes a **dental plan** so that people can take care of their teeth.
10. Women who have a baby can get time off, called **maternity leave**.
11. **Childcare facilities** are offered by companies for people with small children.
12. An extra benefit is often offered as a form of **life insurance**, which helps a spouse or family in the case of death of the wage earner.
13. People working in retail businesses get **employee discounts** as part of their benefit packages.
14. A common perk for senior management is a **company car**.
15. People in companies who often have to entertain clients usually have an **expense account**.
16. When employees fall ill, they can receive **sick pay** until they can return to work.
17. When employees work **flexible hours**, they have a certain amount of freedom to decide when they want to start and finish work.
18. Companies have found that **job sharing** is a way to deal with part-time workers.

Pay and benefits crossword

Type of activity
Information gap

Time
20–30 minutes

Level
Intermediate / B1

Language focus
Defining terms dealing with pay and benefits

Group formation
Whole class, divided into two groups (A and B)

Preparation
Copy the half crosswords A and B so that there are enough for half the class to have A and half to have B.

Lead-in
Brainstorm types of payments and benefits available to employees and elicit collocations such as *dental plan*. Ask students to explain various terms, some of which could be ones they will have to explain when doing the activity.

Activity 1.1 could also be used as a lead-in to this activity.

Procedure
- Divide the class into two groups (A and B) and give crossword A to group A and crossword B to group B.
- Give the groups time to work out definitions of the words they have, so that they can explain the words to the other group. They can either use dictionaries or work with the information from Activity 1.1.
- A and B take turns asking for words. They use language such as *What is 1 across? What is 2 down?* The other group responds with a definition and the first group guesses the word.
- Discuss the answers with the learners (see Introduction).

One-to-one
The teacher and learner have one half of the crossword each and work together to complete it.

Half crossword A

Explain these words to group B.

Across

1 redundancy package
4 employee discounts
7 company car
8 stock options
18 annual salary

Down

2 childcare facilities
6 expense account
14 job sharing
15 pension scheme

Half crossword B

Explain these words to group A.

Across

5 fringe benefits
9 maternity leave
10 flexible hours
17 subsidized canteens

Down

3 performance-related pay
11 sick pay
12 minimum wage
13 life insurance
16 dental plan

Jobs and descriptions

Type of activity
Matching

Time
20–30 minutes

Level
Intermediate / B1

Language focus
Jobs and job descriptions

Group formation
Whole class

Preparation
Copy the cards and cut them up, so that each learner has one business card and one (not matching) job description. If there are six learners in the class, they must have six matching cards between them.

Lead-in
Have a general discussion of companies and departments. Then brainstorm who might work in these departments and what they might do, e.g. a marketing manager works in the marketing department.

Elicit or revise questions about jobs and job responsibilities, such as: *What do you do? Do you work 9–5? Do you work in an office, in a factory?* and responses: *I'm a … I'm responsible for … I'm in charge of … My job is to ensure that …*, etc.

Procedure
- Give each person a business card and a job description, which is not the same as the job on the business card.
- Tell the class they are at an international conference and they should mingle with the other learners. Their goal is to find the person who has the description which matches the job title he or she has got. The learners should ask each other questions based on the descriptions they have, such as *Do you work in the finance department? Are you in charge of human resources?*
- When a learner answers *Yes* to the questions asked, he or she collects the card containing the description of his or her job. He or she then asks the others about the job description he or she has got until he or she has found the person with the job title.
- Learners who have matched their cards can mingle with the others who have finished and introduce themselves and tell the others what they do.
- Discuss the answers with the learners (see Introduction).

Follow-up
Learners choose a business card and describe some of the tasks the person in that job has to do. The others then guess the job.

The teacher can make an OHT of the jobs and the job descriptions. The learners then discuss people they know who have these jobs. They can talk about the job descriptions and add more information if possible.

One-to-one
The learner matches the business cards and descriptions. The teacher can then go on to the follow-up activity described above.

Note
Depending on the size of the class, the teacher can decide which of the cards to use. They might want learners to repeat the activity with different cards at a later date.

This sheet could also be photocopied as is and then cut vertically down the middle, with each half then folded in half. This helps if mingling is difficult and teachers want to let learners read the descriptions and guess the names of the jobs, or vice-versa. This could be done in pairs or small groups.

Vocabulary
promotional materials advertising flyers, brochures, giveaways, etc. which help to make products known to the consumers
recruitment looking for and hiring people to work in the company
sales targets a set amount of items which are expected to be sold

Cards

• Responsible for the overall running of the company • Makes strategic decisions on its behalf	**Gina Hollander** Managing Director **Newcom**	• Organizes all aspects of the running of an office	Bill Smith **Office Manager** Cardston
• Convinces customers to buy the company's products • Must meet sales targets	*Howard Hill* *Sales Representative* KEYSTONE	• Makes sure that products are produced on time • Keeps assembly line working efficiently	**Carl Mayer** Production Manager **ANG**
• Responsible for overseeing the investigation and innovation of new products	***Daniel Rose*** *Research and Development* ***Flower Ltd***	• Responsibilities include deciding on financial strategic direction of the company	JNL Plc Carol Hess Finance Director
• Deals with warehousing and the movement of goods within the company and to and from other companies	George Zell Logistics Manager **Comtech**	• Organizes the distribution of products to branches or to other companies	Karolin Kowalski Distribution Manager **Catty, Inc.**
• Keeps MD's diary, makes arrangements, needs word-processing skills and communication skills	**Anna Klum** PA for Managing Director **Canon Ltd**	• In charge of the development of new computer programs	Josep Gonzalez Software Engineer **Dataform**
• Responsible for advertising campaigns • Oversees the development of promotional materials	Eileen Reiter Marketing Manager HNC	• Deals with the company's software and hardware • Responsible for company network systems	Allan Bean IT Manager **Broadcase, Plc**
• Creates presentations and other artwork for products	April North Graphic designer **BASEtools, INC.**	• Works with customer complaints and customer support	**Janet Fine** Customer Services Representative Paper and Such Ltd.
• Makes sure that products are of the highest quality	Robert Gregson Quality supervisor **The Toy Company**	• Keeps the books, prepares financial reports and works with tax authorities	TEJ Mei Wu Accountant (CA)
• Responsible for recruitment, training and welfare issues of employees	Laurel Jones HR Director ***Zenger, Inc.***	• Makes sure that machines and buildings are in good working order	**Jim Williams** **Maintenance** **Benny Tools Plc**

Words and definitions

Type of activity
Matching

Time
20 minutes

Level
Upper intermediate–Advanced / B2–C1

Language focus
Terms used to describe organizations

Group formation
Individual or pairs

Preparation
Copy the definitions sheet (one for each learner) and fold along the dotted line above the key.

Lead-in
Write on the board two or three terms that are on the sheet. Ask learners if they know the meanings and to give a definition if they do. Explain the terms.

Procedure
- Give out the definitions sheet to the learners and tell them to make sure that the sheet is folded where indicated. Alternatively, cut out all the cards individually.
- Get learners to match the words to their definitions.
- Let learners look at the key to check their work and discuss the results with them (see Introduction).

Follow-up
Learners work in new pairs. They take it in turns to read out a definition for their partner to give them the correct word.

One-to-one
Begin a discussion about the company the learner works for. Elicit words used to describe it. Then have the leaner fill out the sheet and discuss it with you.

Definitions

1 money earned after all expenses have been paid	**a** *stock exchange*
2 a report showing the financial transactions of a company	**b** *bankruptcy*
3 money, assets and property belonging to a business	**c** *unlimited liability*
4 the equal parts into which a company divides its capital	**d** *annual report*
5 the place where shares are traded	**e** *volunteer*
6 the money, provided by shareholders or loans, that a company has at its disposal	**f** *capital*
7 money given to charities or non-profit organizations	**g** *charity*
8 directors' report on a company's finances, made public at the end of a financial year	**h** *limited liability*
9 the legal situation when a company is not able to pay its debts	**i** *profit*
10 a person who works for an organization without being paid	**j** *fund-raising*
11 the act of forming a registered company	**k** *finances*
12 a non-profit organization set up to help people in need	**l** *to trade shares*
13 the act of collecting money for a cause or a non-profit organization	**m** *industry*
14 the situation where an owner or partner of a company is responsible for all debts created by the company, with no limit as to how much must be paid	**n** *share capital*
15 the situation where owners of a company are not responsible for all the debts of the company	**o** *NGO*
16 a person who holds shares in a company	**p** *shares*
17 the total value of the assets of a company, which are held as shares	**q** *incorporation*
18 to buy and sell shares	**r** *statement of account*
19 businesses involved in the processing and/or production of goods	**s** *shareholder*
20 a non-profit, voluntary citizens' group, organized on a local, national or international level and not run by a government	**t** *donations*

Fold here

Key

1 i 2 r 3 f 4 p 5 a 6 k 7 t 8 d 9 b 10 e 11 q 12 g 13 j 14 c 15 h
16 s 17 n 18 l 19 m 20 o

Characteristics of organizations

Type of activity
Categorizing

Time
15–20 minutes

Level
Upper intermediate–Advanced / B2–C1

Language focus
Types of organization

Group formation
Pairs or small groups

Preparation
Copy the organization grid, one for each learner.

Copy one set of the cards for each group of learners.

Lead-in
Brainstorm types of organization and ask learners what they know about different types. If they are in work, ask what kind of organization theirs is.

Activity 2.1 could also be used as a lead-in to this activity.

Procedure
- Divide the class into pairs or small groups and give out the organization cards and the information cards.
- Instruct the learners to find the cards which belong to each type of organization and place them on the grid. Tell the learners that there are four cards for each type of organization and point out that two information cards are the same as two of the organization types share a common feature.
- Discuss the answers with the learners (see Introduction) and get them to write the information into the correct part of the grid.

Follow-up
Learners write questions about the different organizations to ask the other groups.

Learners find additional information about these organizational forms and add this information to the grid.

Learners discuss the types of companies they work for. As different countries have different laws regarding companies and firms, it is not always possible to translate the word for a particular type of company directly into English. The learners should try to decide which aspects of these firms most closely apply to the companies they work for.

One-to-one
The teacher discusses the learner's company and the type of organization it is. The learner completes the grid. The learner can then make a mini-presentation of his or her company.

Types of organization

Sole trader	Private limited company (Ltd)	Public limited company (plc)	Non-profit organization	Public corporation

Cards

Sole trader	Private limited company (Ltd)	Public limited company (plc)	Non-profit organization	Public corporation
is owned and managed by one person	shares cannot be bought by the general public	shares can be sold to the general public	relies on volunteers but is managed by paid professionals	is owned and financed by the state
owner has unlimited liability in the case of bankruptcy	shareholders keep control of company	shares can be traded on the stock exchange	puts effort into fund-raising and receiving donations	includes nationalized industries
finances are private and the company is usually small	company has limited liability	company has limited liability	often a charity or service organization	board of directors is appointed by government
owner receives all the profits from the company	no minimum amount of share capital is required at time of set up	a minimum amount of £50,000 share capital is required at time of incorporation	often an NGO (non-governmental organization)	produces annual reports and statements of accounts but does not have to make a profit

Co-operative crossword

Type of activity
Information gap

Time
20–30 minutes

Level
Upper intermediate–Advanced / B2–C1

Language focus
Organizations and how they are set up

Group formation
Groups of four

Preparation
Make a copy of the crossword for each learner and fold the sheet along the dotted line above the key.

Copy the clues, a different set, A, B, C or D, for each learner.

Lead-in
Write out several of the types of organization from Activity 2.2 on the board and ask learners what they know about them. Alternatively, words describing organizations can be put on the board and learners can try to find definitions for them. They can go on to discuss organizations they are familiar with themselves.

Activity 2.1 and/or 2.2 could also be used as lead-ins to this activity.

Procedure
- Divide the class into groups of four and give each person in the group a blank crossword and his or her own set of clues (A, B, C or D). Tell them to make sure that the sheet with the crossword is folded where indicated.
- In order to solve the puzzle, each group member reads his or her clue aloud. The clues are written in such a way that it is necessary for the learners to listen to each other's clues in order to solve the puzzle.
- Discuss the answers with the learners (see Introduction).

Follow-up
Learners can make up their own definitions of the various words and ask the others to guess which word they mean.

One-to-one
The learner and teacher can work with two sets of clues each.

Note
If the class does not divide evenly into groups of four, learners can share a set of clues or a group of three, for example, can have the A, B and C clues and read the last set of clues together.

Crossword clues A

Across

1 This can consist of money or other assets.
4 It starts with B.
8 This includes nationalized industries.
10 Owners of a company are responsible for any debts.
12 It starts with D.
14 Its shares are not bought by the public.
15 This person owns part of a public company.
16 This may be an international or a national organization.

Down

2 This is printed.
3 The second word starts with L.
5 This is a type of company.
6 This is found in several large cities around the world.
7 This is a way to start a company.
9 Owners of a company are responsible for only part of any debts incurred by the company.
11 The owner has unlimited liability.
13 This person works for organizations he or she believes in.

Crossword clues B

Across

1 This is needed to start a business.
4 It is a noun.
8 This organization does not have to make a profit.
10 The first word starts with U.
12 This has to do with money.
14 The first word starts with P.
15 This person might make or lose money.
16 This organization helps people.

Down

2 This must appear once a year.
3 Its shares can be traded on the stock exchange.
5 This company does not pay taxes.
6 The first word starts with S.
7 This involves many legal requirements.
9 Private property of company owners is protected.
11 The owner receives all the profits.
13 This person is not paid to work.

Crossword clues C

Across

1 It is a noun.
4 This occurs when a company is having serious financial problems.
8 This company is owned by the state.
10 Private possessions may not be protected if a company fails.
12 It is a noun.
14 One of the words can be abbreviated to *Ltd.*
15 It starts with S.
16 This organization has many people who work without being paid.

Down

2 This is approved by the board of directors.
3 This organization must have a specific amount of minimum capital (held as shares) when it is set up.
5 This company does not make a profit.
6 This has to do with buying and selling.
7 After this, a company becomes official.
9 Both words begin with L.
11 The first word starts with S.
13 It starts with V.

Crossword clues D

Across

1 It starts with C.
4 The situation when a company is unable to make payments.
8 Its board of directors is appointed by the government.
10 There is no limit regarding the amount of debt which must be paid.
12 This is a type of gift.
14 This company must have less than a specific amount of share capital when it is founded.
15 This person receives the company's annual report.
16 This organization often does fund-raising.

Down

2 This information is public.
3 This is often abbreviated to *plc.*
5 This may be an NGO.
6 The second word starts with E.
7 It starts with I.
9 This is found in both PLCs and limited companies.
11 Its owner has no partners.
13 This person may work for a charity.

Crossword

Fold here

Key

Phone dialogues

Type of activity
Sorting and ordering

Time
20 minutes

Level
Intermediate–Upper intermediate / B1–B2

Language focus
Telephoning language

Group formation
Pairs or small groups

Preparation
Make a copy of the three dialogues for each group of learners and cut them into strips.

Lead-in
Find out how many learners make or receive phone calls in English and discuss how often they need to do this. Brainstorm what sorts of phone conversations these are.

Tell the learners that they are going to look at three telephone conversations: one to a forwarding company, one to a bank and one to a hotel. Elicit all the reasons why you might phone those places and write them on the board.

Procedure
- Divide the class into pairs or small groups and give out all the dialogue strips.
- Tell the learners that these strips deal with three different phone dialogues, which need to be sorted and put into order. (If dealing with three activities at once seems too challenging, give out the dialogues one at a time and get the learners to put each in order separately.)
- Point out that each dialogue is marked to show the beginning and the ending.

Alternative
- Give the strips of one of the dialogues to the class and have each person decide if the strip he or she has is something said by the caller or by the receiver of the call. Then tell the callers to stand at one side of the room and the receivers at the other.
- The person with *Beginning* on his or her card starts by reading his or her strip. Then the person from the other side who thinks they have the next line continues. This goes on until the group has completed the dialogue.
- Discuss the answers with the learners (see Introduction).

Follow-up
Learners role play the dialogues in pairs.

Learners write their own dialogues which they cut into strips and give to other learners to put together.

One-to-one
The teacher gives the strips for the dialogues to the learner and the learner sorts them and puts them in order. They discuss the types of phone calls the learner has to make and see which language in the dialogues would be useful for him or her.

Note
Learners can be given the information that Dialogue 1 is about a missing delivery and has 11 strips, Dialogue 2 is about making an appointment and has 10 strips and Dialogue 3 is about giving information to a hotel about a late arrival and has 11 strips.

Vocabulary
to be due in at when someone or something is expected to arrive
to call up on the computer to bring data onto the computer screen in order to look at it
corporate loan a loan from a bank made to a company
current status the situation now (in this case, the whereabouts of a shipment)
delivery goods which are brought to a customer or place of business or manufacturer
dispatch department the department in a company responsible for physically sending out goods
to put a trace on something to find out where something is at a particular moment
shipping the physical sending of goods
shuttle a vehicle that regularly travels between two places
supplier the company or person where a business buys the goods it needs

Dialogues

1

IMC Forwarding Company, can I help you?	**(1 – Beginning)**
Hello, I'm calling from UL Electronics. We're having a problem with a late delivery.	
I'll put you through to our dispatch department. Just hold on a minute.	
Dispatch department, Mary speaking. What can I do for you?	
This is Bob Jonas at UL Electronics. We've been waiting for a delivery from our supplier in Manchester. I phoned them but they said that you're responsible for the shipping.	
Just a moment, Mr Jonas, I'll have to check. Can you give me the order number?	
Yes, it's RN5 3769.	
I'm just calling it up on the computer. That was RN5 3769? Yes, here it is. I can't see the current status but I'll put a trace on it. Can you give me a phone number where I can reach you, Mr Jonas?	
Yes, my office number's 0345 69 63 49.	
Let me repeat that: 0345 69 63 49. I'll phone you as soon as I've got any information about your delivery.	
Thanks so much. I'll be expecting your call. Goodbye.	**(1 – Ending)**

2

Central Bank, Patricia Smith's office.	**(2 – Beginning)**
Hello, this is Jośe Senna. I'd like to speak to Ms Smith.	
May I ask what it's about?	
Yes, I'm Head of the Finance department at TK Textiles, and we'd like to discuss a corporate loan in order to expand our operations abroad.	
I see. Well, this is Ms Smith's area, but I'm afraid she's going to be tied up most of the day. Would you like to make an appointment with her?	
I think that's a good idea as there's quite a bit to discuss. I've got some time on Thursday afternoon.	
Just a second, let me check her diary. Oh, I'm afraid that she'll be out of town on Thursday. How about Wednesday?	
Wednesday late morning would be fine. I could get to her office by 11.00 a.m.	
OK, Mr Senna, I've got you scheduled for 11.00 a.m. on Wednesday.	
OK. See you on Wednesday, then.	**(2 – Ending)**

3

Regency Hotel, good afternoon.	**(3 – Beginning)**
I'm calling about a reservation.	
Yes, can I take your name?	
This is Amélie Thiriau from Paul O'Brien's office. He asked me to call and let you know that he'll be arriving later than planned.	
Just a moment, Ms Thiriau. I'm just checking the reservation. Yes, he was due in at 8 p.m. and should be picked up by our shuttle service at the airport.	
That's why I'm calling. His flight's been delayed and he won't be landing till 9.30. Can you let your shuttle bus driver know about this so that he won't have to wait too long at the airport?	
Yes, of course. We've usually got a shuttle once an hour but our last arrival today was scheduled for 8.30. I'll tell our driver as soon as he comes that he'll need to make another trip. I've got all the flight information here, so we already know which terminal to make the pick-up at.	
That'd be great. He'll be waiting for your driver then. Can you also ask him to phone his office tomorrow morning before he leaves the hotel?	
No problem. I'll let him know that you phoned and tell him to call you in the morning.	
Thanks so much. You've been very helpful.	
You're welcome. Have a nice evening.	**(3 – Ending)**

Phone phrases

Type of activity
Four in a row (noughts and crosses) game

Time
20–30 minutes

Level
Intermediate–Upper intermediate / B1–B2

Language focus
Telephoning language

Group formation
Pairs

Preparation
Copy the four in a row sheet for each learner.

Have a dice for each pair of learners.

Lead-in
Brainstorm standard telephone phrases and responses with the learners. Give some phrases from the game as examples.

Activity 3.1 could also be used as a lead-in to this activity.

Procedure
- Divide the class into pairs and give each pair a dice and give each player a copy of the Four in a row board.
- Have the pairs decide which person in each pair will use the symbol X and which will use the symbol O to mark their sheet.
- Instruct the learners to take it in turns to roll the dice and choose one of the squares from the column which corresponds to the number on the dice. They must then follow the instruction in the square, e.g. use appropriate language for a specific situation (such as ask or respond to a question) or fill in a missing word in a typical telephone phrase.
- If a learner gives a correct answer, he or she marks that particular square (which cannot be used again) using either the X or the O that they previously agreed on. This works best if they mark both sheets, not just their own, and also tick off the numbers at the top which have already been chosen.
- The learners have to decide between themselves if an answer is correct or not. If they have a problem, they can ask for help from the teacher.
- When one learner has got four Os or four Xs in a vertical, horizontal or diagonal row, he or she is the winner of the game.

Follow-up
Learners look at all the squares which didn't come up in the game and follow the instructions. This can be done as a whole-class activity, with the teacher calling out a number and a learner's name and asking the learner to come up with the correct response.

One-to-one
The teacher can play this game with the learner.

Note
Some groups may be more comfortable having the answer sheets so that they can check if their partner has answered the question correctly. Just remind them that these are only suggestions and they can check with you if they are unsure about an answer.

Four in a row board

⚀	⚁	⚂	⚃	⚄	⚅
1 7 13 19 25 31	2 8 14 20 26 32	3 9 15 21 27 33	4 10 16 22 28 34	5 11 17 23 29 35	6 12 18 24 30 36

1 Call a business partner and introduce yourself.	**2** May I ask who's calling?	**3** Let the caller know that the person they want has answered the phone.	**4** Could you spell your name for me, please?	**5** Call a hotel you left this morning to ask if you left your diary behind in the room.	**6** Would you like to leave a message?
7 Call a travel agent to reserve a flight to New York next Tuesday.	**8** She's out at the moment. Can she reach you this afternoon?	**9** Call your office and ask if anyone phoned while you were out.	**10** I'm afraid he's got the day off. Can someone else help you?	**11** I'm afraid that she's tied __________ at the moment.	**12** Phone Directory Enquiries and ask for the number of the Central Bank in Milan.
13 Explain to a caller that your boss can't speak at the moment.	**14** Could you tell me your phone number?	**15** Thanks for __________.	**16** Ask to speak to the sales department about your order.	**17** Call your bank and explain that you haven't received your new credit card yet.	**18** Call a restaurant to make a reservation for a business lunch.
19 The person you want is busy. Leave a message on their voicemail.	**20** Offer to take a message for a colleague.	**21** Call an airline to ask when a flight is supposed to arrive.	**22** I'll tell him to call you back. How long will you be at your desk?	**23** Sales Department, Carol Jones __________. Can I help you?	**24** Explain that your colleague has the day off. Offer to help.
25 Arrange to meet a visitor at the airport.	**26** Phone a supplier about a late delivery.	**27** He's in a meeting. Can you call later?	**28** May I ask what __________ is about?	**29** You would like to invite a business partner for dinner next week.	**30** Find out what a business partner would like to do in the evening.
31 Phone home to say that you have to work late.	**32** Offer to put a call through to your boss, George Vida.	**33** Ask a caller to phone later that day.	**34** The line is busy. Would you like to hold?	**35** Ask a caller to repeat his or her name.	**36** Her line is __________. Can you hold for a few minutes?

Key

(possible answers)

1 Hello, my name is Joan McKearny and I am calling from Perry's in Dublin.	**2** Yes, this is Bill Beard.	**3** Speaking.	**4** J-E-A-N S-M-I-double T-Y.	**5** I'm calling to ask if you found my diary in room 312. I was there last night.	**6** Yes, please tell her that Carolyn Dunne called.
7 I would like to book a flight to New York next Tuesday.	**8** Yes, I'll be in my office. / No, I will be out all afternoon.	**9** It's Bob here. Has anyone called since I left the office?	**10** No, I need to speak to him. / Yes, can you connect me to his boss?	**11** I'm afraid that she's tied **up** at the moment.	**12** I would like the number for the Central Bank in Milan, please.
13 I'm afraid she's quite busy at the moment.	**14** Yes, it's 303-414-6903.	**15** Thanks for **calling**. / Thanks for **your help**.	**16** I would like to speak to a sales representative about our order.	**17** My credit card hasn't arrived. Has it been sent to me?	**18** I would like to book a table for 12.00 tomorrow for three people. The name is Jones.
19 Hi, Mike, it's Cindy here. Can you call me back later, please? My number is 01326 954 787.	**20** He/She is busy at the moment. May I take a message for him/her?	**21** Can you tell me when the flight from Liverpool is due in?	**22** I'll be here for several hours.	**23** Sales Department, Carol Jones **speaking**. Can I help you?	**24** My colleague is off today. Can I help you?
25 I'll be at the airport at 6.00 p.m. to meet you.	**26** Our delivery hasn't arrived yet. Can you check on it?	**27** Yes, when would be a good time?	**28** May I ask what **it** is about?	**29** Have you got time for dinner next week?	**30** What would you like to do this evening?
31 I'm afraid I'm going to be late this evening.	**32** I can connect you to George / Mr Vida if you like.	**33** Could you phone again this afternoon, after 4 p.m.?	**34** Yes, I'll hold. / No, I'll call back later.	**35** Could you repeat that, please?	**36** Her line is **engaged/busy**. Can you hold for a few minutes?

Addresses

Type of activity
Exchanging information

Time
10–20 minutes

Level
Pre-intermediate / B1

Language focus
The alphabet and symbols/punctuation used in email addresses

Group formation
Whole class

Preparation
Copy and cut up the business cards.

Lead-in
Discuss with the learners what their experience of emailing is, for example how often they email and what kind of problems they have.

Write this email address on the board:

charlieSmith@sales_new-mail.com.uk

and elicit how email terms and symbols/punctuation are spoken:

charlieSmith	all one word
c	small *c*
S	capital *s*
@	at
_	underscore
-	hyphen
.	dot

The address above could be given as:

charlieSmith, all one word, small c, h, a, r, l, i, e, capital s, small m, i, t, h, at sales, underscore new, hyphen mail, dot com, dot u, k.

Point out that *lower case* is often used for *small* and, less commonly, *upper case* for *capital*. Note that what comes after *dot* is sometimes spoken as a word – com, co, org, gov – and sometimes as letters – fr (f, r) de (d, e).

You could also go through the letters of the alphabet to check that the learners know how to say them correctly.

Then practise by getting learners to choose six letters of the alphabet or symbols/punctuation and write them on a piece of paper. You then call out letters and symbols/punctuation in random order until someone has marked off the six he or she has chosen. This person then calls out *Bingo*.

These introductory phrases should also be elicited, revised or pre-taught: *Hello, my name's … How do you spell that? What's your name? What's your email address? Can I have your email address? Sorry? What was that again? Can you just repeat that?*

Procedure
- Give a card to each person in the class and tell them that they are at a conference or business meeting.
- Each person should walk around the room and write down as many names and email addresses as possible within the time limit you set. Depending on the size of the class and the amount of practice you feel they need, you can set a time limit of 10–15 minutes.
- In smaller classes, give each person more than one card.
- In larger classes, make more than one set of the cards. These could be on different coloured paper and learners can then be instructed to work with those who have the same coloured cards as they do, to avoid duplicate addresses.
- Discuss the answers with the learners (see Introduction). Learners can use what they wrote to say the names and addresses for you and the others to check.

Follow-up
Ask learners to bring business cards to class and practise saying the email addresses to each other.

One-to-one
Ask the learner if he or she has got any business cards which you can use to practise saying and spelling the email addresses. Then work with these cards to make sure that the learner can accurately say and write the email addresses.

Business cards

Bob Brown
Graphic Artist
b.brown@lol.com

George Wilson
Project Manager
Wilson1@mr.mil

Karen Woods
Professor of Medicine
KW@ghuni_edu

Hugh Carstairs
Chairman of the Board
Carst@ecofriendly.org.lk

Samuel Wien
Engineering Consultant
S_Wien@khu.id

Helga Holler
Chief Bookkeeper
Helga.Holler@statehouse.gov

Josef Weiss
Deputy Mayor
JoW@mnr-me.gv.an

Rose Mueller
Reservations Clerk
Rosi-M@pension-mueller.se

Fred Parson
Logistics Manager
FRED.PARSON@MAILUSA.COM

Andreas Baker
Sales Representative
andreas-baker@limo-rsa.ilt

Jia Li Chang
Export Manager
ChangJL@nel.cno

Aakarshan Sharman
Marketing Coordinator
Aak/Sharmy@provi.int

4.2 Email styles

Type of activity
Sorting and ordering

Time
15 minutes

Level
Pre-intermediate–Intermediate / B1

Language focus
Formal and informal phrases for emails

Group formation
Pairs or small groups

Preparation
Copy the two emails and cut them into strips, one set for each group of learners.

Lead-in
Ask learners about their email habits. Who do they write to? How formal are their emails? Do they find that they are more formal in English than in their own language? Explain that both formal and informal emails are common in the business world.

Procedure
- Divide the class into pairs or small groups and give a set of strips to each group.
- Tell the learners that there are two emails referring to setting up a lunch date, one of them to a business partner (formal) and the other to a friend (informal). The groups should use the style of language to help them decide which strips belong together.
- The group puts each email together in order. Tell the learners that more than one order is possible, apart from the beginning and ending of the emails.
- Discuss the answers with the learners (see Introduction). Ask groups to talk about what makes some phrases more formal than others (vocabulary, full sentences, last names/first names, full forms/contractions, etc.).

One-to-one
The teacher leads in with a discussion about the types of emails the learner writes. Then the teacher gives the learner the strips and has him or her put the emails together. They discuss both emails and which are more common for the learner.

Note
Several of the sentences can be in a different order as long as the email makes sense.

Informal email

Re: Getting together in August
Hi Jane
Thanks for the email about your new job in New York. It was great hearing from you.
I just wanted to let you know that I'll be coming to New York in the first week of July and would love to meet for lunch.
You can pick the day and the place. I'm totally flexible as I haven't made many plans yet.
Just send me a quick note and let me know where and when to meet you.
Take a look at the photos I've attached – I think you will recognize lots of people.
Shall I bring some of that chocolate you like so much?
Take care and see you in a couple of months. I'm really looking forward to getting together and catching up.
Love
Susan

Formal email

Re: Lunch meeting
Dear Ms Turner
Thank you for your email and your inquiry about our new product line.
I am writing to inform you that I will be in your area in the last week of July and would like to invite you to lunch so that we can discuss these matters in person.
Please let me know if this would be convenient for you and if there is a day you would prefer.
As I will be out of the office until then, I will ask my assistant to phone you and confirm the time and place.
I have attached some information which I think will be of interest to you.
Let me know if there is anything in particular which you would need before our meeting.
I am looking forward to meeting you.
Sincerely
Carol Brown

Making an arrangement

Type of activity

Matching and ordering

Time

15 minutes

Level

Pre-intermediate–Intermediate / B1

Language focus

Functions and formal and informal phrases for emails

Group formation

Individual or pairs

Preparation

Copy and cut up one sheet for each learner.

Lead-in

Ask learners about their email habits. Who do they write to? How formal are their emails? Do they find that they are more formal in English than in their own language? Explain that both formal and informal emails are common in the business world.

Activity 4.2 could also be used as a lead-in to this activity.

Procedure

- Divide the class into pairs or do this as an individual activity. Give the sheets to the learners.
- Go through the functions and check that the learners know what they mean.
- Tell the learners that they need to do two things: decide what the function of each pair of formal and informal sentences is and write it in the Function column; decide on the best order for the emails and write the appropriate number in the Order column.
- Discuss the answers with the learners (see Introduction).

Follow-up

The learners work in pairs and each pair chooses one of these topics: setting up an appointment or asking for information about a product. They then write a formal email about this particular subject. The group then exchanges the email with another of the pairs, who rewrites the email in an informal style, keeping the meaning the same. These two emails are then given to two other pairs, who have to take turns answering the emails in the same styles. In the end, each of the pairs writes a formal email, changes an email into an informal style and answers a formal and an informal email.

This activity would take about 45 minutes and is recommended for learners who have to do a lot of email writing in their jobs.

One-to-one

The learner completes the sheet and discusses it with the teacher.

Note

Several of the sentences can be in a different order as long as the email makes sense.

Email arrangement

Functions

Subject
Salutation
Answering a forwarded email
Reference (to an earlier email)
Apology
Giving information
Making an appointment
Request
Attachment information Offering help
Offering help
Asking for confirmation
Closing remarks
Complimentary closing

Order	Function	Formal	Informal
		I have reserved a table at the Four Seasons on October 16 at 12.30.	How about The Four Seasons, say 12.30? You liked it last time.
		Please inform me if there is anything I can help you with before our meeting.	Just send me a quick note if you have any other questions before we meet.
		Can you confirm by Friday if you will be able to come?	Can you let me know by Friday if this is OK for you?
		You will find the latest information for suppliers in the attachment.	I'm attaching some supplier information that I thought you'd like to see.
		Please accept my apologies for the delay in replying.	I'm really sorry that I haven't replied before now.
		Re: Lunch on Friday, October 16	Re: Lunch on 16/10?
		I am looking forward to your reply.	Hope to hear from you soon.
		I would greatly appreciate it if you could send me specific information about the proposal before our meeting.	It'd be a help to get some of your ideas about the proposal before we meet.
		Yours sincerely	Bye for now
		Dear Mr Turner	Hi Jack
		Thank you for your interest in our company and the information about your upcoming visit.	Thanks for letting us know you'll be here next week and we're glad you want to find out more about us.
		Ms Johns has forwarded your email to me and asked me to reply to it.	Carol just sent this on to me and asked me to get in touch with you.
		I am writing to inform you that we are setting up a lunch with several people interested in your business proposal.	Just wanted to let you know that lunch would be great. A couple of us would like to discuss your ideas in person.

Key

Order	Function	Formal	Informal
1	**Subject**	Re: Lunch on Friday, October 16	Re: Lunch on 16/10?
2	**Salutation**	Dear Mr Turner	Hi Jack
3	**Answering a forwarded email**	Ms Johns has forwarded your email to me and asked me to reply to it.	Carol just sent this on to me and asked me to get in touch with you.
4	**Reference (to an earlier email)**	Thank you for your interest in our company and the information about your upcoming visit.	Thanks for letting us know you'll be here next week and we're glad you want to find out more about us.
5	**Apology**	Please accept my apologies for the delay in replying.	I'm really sorry that I haven't replied before now.
6	**Giving information**	I am writing to inform you that we are setting up a lunch with several people interested in your business proposal.	Just wanted to let you know that lunch would be great. A couple of us would like to discuss your ideas in person.
7	**Making an appointment**	I have reserved a table at the Four Seasons on October 16 at 12.30.	How about The Four Seasons, say 12.30? You liked it last time.
8	**Request**	I would greatly appreciate it if you could send me specific information about the proposal before our meeting.	It'd be a help to get some of your ideas about the proposal before we meet.
9	**Attachment information**	You will find the latest information for suppliers in the attachment.	I'm attaching some supplier information that I thought you'd like to see.
10	**Offering help**	Please inform me if there is anything I can help you with before our meeting.	Just send me a quick note if you have any other questions before we meet.
11	**Asking for confirmation**	Can you confirm by Friday if you will be able to come?	Can you let me know by Friday if this is OK for you?
12	**Closing remarks**	I am looking forward to your reply.	Hope to hear from you soon.
13	**Complimentary closing**	Yours sincerely	Bye for now

Hard and soft sell

Type of activity
Ordering

Time
20 minutes

Level
Upper intermediate–Advanced / B2–C1

Language focus
Sales pitches

Group formation
Pairs or small groups

Preparation
Copy and cut up the soft sell and hard sell cards for each group.

Copy the aspects of language table for each learner.

Lead-in
Tell learners that they should imagine that they have a product to sell in a new market. They should discuss the type of language they would use and their ultimate goals. Do they want to establish a long-term customer base or do they want to sell their product as quickly as possible? Brainstorm typical sales phrases and ask them which of these two categories the phrases fit better into (soft sell / customer-oriented language for the long term or hard sell / sales-oriented language for quick sales). Prompt them if necessary with one or two phrases from the cards.

Procedure
- Divide the class into pairs or small groups and give out the cards with the phrases, but not the aspects of language table.
- Tell the learners to divide the phrases into the two categories of hard sell (sales-oriented) and soft sell (customer-oriented) language.
- Discuss the answers with the learners (see Introduction). Ask learners to think about what makes the phrases more customer-oriented or more sales-oriented from a language point of view.
- Give out the table detailing the aspects of the two types of language and go through them.

Follow-up
Learners can write their own phrases and discuss the situations they would use them in.

One-to-one
The teacher gives the cards to the learner to classify and they discuss the language together afterwards.

Note
Encourage discussion of sales techniques: the ultimate goal of all salespeople is to make a sale. There are different factors, however, which contribute to 'softer' or 'harder' sales. In some cases, salespeople will be working with their customers for a longer period of time and therefore it is more necessary to set up a long-term relationship with them. In other cases, the chance to make a sale may only be at the moment of selling and therefore the hard sell approach may be more appropriate. This is an issue which top salespeople are familiar with – they often have to judge on the spot which way to approach a sale. They have to be able to adapt to the buyer and may have to change tactics in the middle of the sales pitch. Closing the deal depends to a large extent on the intuition of the salesperson.

Cards

Soft sell (more customer-oriented)	Hard sell (more sales-oriented)
I get the feeling that you and I are very much alike.	I know that a product like this is just what you need.
I think we share the same opinion about this type of product.	I am sure that this product will make your life easier.
Your satisfaction with this product is very important to me.	This product is without doubt one of the best on the market.
Haven't we all been hoping for such an invention?	You don't have to look around. I guarantee you won't find a better product at a better price.
I would be very interested in knowing what you think about this product.	I've been selling these products for years and I tell you that you can't go wrong with them.
Something tells me that our interests are very similar.	Do you think you will get a better deal elsewhere?
Tell me what is important for you when you make a purchase such as this one.	If you don't buy this product today, I'm sure you'll regret it.
Have you got any questions which I haven't answered yet?	Today is the last day of the special deal. Next week it will cost considerably more.
Have you seen for yourself how this product can make things easier for you?	If you wait to decide, you will really miss out on the opportunity of a lifetime.
Would you like to hear anything else about the benefits of this product?	I can't possibly sell this product any cheaper.
Have you got any concerns I haven't addressed yet?	I have a limited number of these products left so you must decide as soon as possible if you want to buy one.

Aspects of more customer-oriented language	**Aspects of more sales-oriented language**
The soft-sell approach persuades people by encouraging them, by doing the following:	The hard-sell approach uses every effort to convince a customer to buy a product, by doing the following:
Using phrases such as *I think ... I get the feeling ... Something tells me that ... Tell me what is important*	Using phrases such as *I am sure ... I guarantee ... You can't go wrong with ... If you wait ...*
Asking questions for which you expect an answer.	Asking questions for which you don't expect an answer.
Getting the opinion of the customer.	Giving your own opinion.
Finding out what the customer would like.	Indicating that you know more than the customer.
Giving the customer time.	Putting time pressure on the customer.

The marketplace

Type of activity
Role play

Time
30–40 minutes

Level
Upper intermediate–Advanced / B2–C1

Language focus
Language for buying and selling products

Group formation
Whole class

Preparation
Copy and cut up the role play instruction cards, one of the two cards for each salesperson.

Copy and cut up the product cards, one card for each salesperson.

Lead-in
Begin by asking learners if they have ever been convinced by a salesperson to buy something they didn't plan to buy or even really need. Try to elicit from them what made them buy the product: the quality of the product, the price, sympathy for the salesperson, interest, curiosity, etc.

Activity 5.1 could also be used as a lead-in to this activity.

Procedure
- Divide the class into two groups. One group will be the salespeople and the other the buyers. Divide the salespeople again into two groups, customer-oriented and sales-oriented.
- Tell the buyers (out-of-hearing of the salespeople) that each of them has got 600 units of local currency to spend on various interesting products.
- Tell the salespeople that each of the products they have to sell costs 100 units of the local currency but they can offer up to a 25% discount (making the price 75 units) if they feel it will help them to sell their products. They will be judged, however, on how many units they can collect, and the person with the most units is the winner of the game. This is also out-of-hearing of the buyers.
- Give out the product cards to the salespeople.
- Give the 'customer-oriented' role cards to half of the group of salespeople and the 'sales-oriented' role cards to the other half. Give the salespeople some time to think of two or three special features and benefits of their products.
- Tell the buyers to sit with two or three other buyers and discuss the types of new products they would like to see on the market and the features and benefits they would like to get from them. Give them one or two ideas along the lines of the products on the cards to get them thinking in terms of gadgets. They can also discuss what makes a salesperson trustworthy or believable.
- Open the marketplace and tell the salespeople that they should find a buyer and begin to talk to him or her about the products they have for sale (choosing the ones they think most suitable for that person). Set a time limit of 15–25 minutes and make it clear that the salespeople should try to talk to at least three or four buyers. At the end of the time, ask the buyers how much they spent and what they bought. Ask them why they bought products from specific people. Then ask the salespeople how much they earned. Ask them to describe their sales strategies and whether they found it easy or difficult to sell their products.
- Reveal to the class which salespeople were sales-oriented and which were customer-oriented. Get the learners to discuss what differences they noticed in the two styles.

One-to-one
The learner can choose one of the salesperson roles (without telling the teacher which one until the end of the activity) and sell products to the teacher. The teacher can decide if the learner used appropriate language depending on which role he or she chose.

Note
This activity is designed to make learners aware of the value of rapport with customers. Normally, people tend to be more comfortable with those who can establish rapport and appear to be understanding and sympathetic to their needs. Some people are, however, influenced by salespeople who pressure them, but they are not always happy about this. The reflection time at the end of the activity is very important, and time should be left to discuss issues that arose during the game.

It is also important for learners to recognize the different sales situations which arise. In situations where a long-term relationship with the buyer can mean sales in the future, a salesperson may act differently from the way they act in a situation in which they probably won't see the buyer again.

Role cards

Customer-oriented salesperson

Do everything you can to establish a relationship with the potential buyer. Try to match body language (without being obvious). Be understanding, helpful and friendly. Ask real questions and listen carefully to the answers. Try and put yourself in the other person's shoes. Don't offer your opinion too frequently; listen to what the buyer says.

Sales-oriented salesperson

Do everything you can to convince your partners that they cannot live without your product. You indicate that you know much more than the buyer and that you feel it necessary to show your superiority to him or to her. Try to use different body language than your partner does. Ask more rhetorical questions (for which you don't expect an answer) and give your opinion freely. Do most of the talking.

The Wonder Car

The latest in GPS – this car is equipped with a special 'parking place' finder. It electronically senses where there is a free space and tells you how to drive there. Never have problems parking your car again!

The Meeting Saver

This product always knows what you should say at meetings. You can daydream or think about other things and when the group looks at you, the Meeting Saver shows the proper response on a small screen. It looks like a palm pilot so no one will notice it at a meeting as anything unusual.

The Clothes Organizer

You have an important day in front of you and don't know what to wear. Type in the sort of occasion, and the Clothes Organizer pulls the correct clothing out of your wardrobe, including matching socks. It then cleans and irons the clothes and polishes your shoes. Never arrive wearing the wrong clothes again!

The Tax Helper

Do you have problems organizing your receipts? Use the Tax Helper to finish off your yearly tax returns in no time. Put your receipts inside the special machine attached to your PC and start the program.

They will be sorted, numbered and entered into a spreadsheet program. Finally, your finished tax return will come out of your computer.

€ € € € € € € € € € €

The Talking Map

Do you have trouble reading maps? With the Talking Map you only need to point to the place where you are and the place you want to go to, and the map will tell you exactly how to get there. It also turns itself in the correct direction. The special thing about this map is whichever way you hold it, the writing on it is always the right way up.

The Forever Full Fridge

Never run out of milk or butter again. This fridge is linked to a delivery service at your local supermarket. Just put the products in their specially-marked places. When they begin to run out, the fridge automatically sends an electronic message to the shop and the products are delivered within the hour.

Pet Friend

Busy people don't always have time for their pets. The dog walker/cat feeder can take your dog out for a walk and even clean up the mess. It can also be programmed to feed your cat. Enjoy your pets without the work.

Super Cleaner

Wouldn't you like to come home to a neat and tidy flat every night? This marvellous machine not only puts your dishes in the dishwasher, it also organizes the papers on your desk, stacks the newspapers, washes the floor, cleans the windows and makes the bed. Once you have tried this out, you will never want to live without one again!

The Best Answerphone in the World!

This answerphone has got a voice recognition function which allows it to give callers personalized messages. You only need to type in a list of names and the information that these people should be given. Then when they call, they hear a message designed just for them.

Oven Chef

Do you have time to cook? If not, just send the Oven Chef a text message with the menu you would like to have. When you get home, the food will be ready.

Mood Radio

Most people like certain music at certain times. This radio senses how you are feeling and automatically plays the music which suits your mood best. If you don't feel like music at all, it switches itself off.

Email Reader

Are you overwhelmed by your emails? Use the Email Reader to sort and prioritize your emails. It puts the important ones at the top of the list, puts the unimportant ones at the bottom and automatically opens the ones with jokes when it senses you need a laugh.

The marketing mix

Type of activity

Ordering

Time

20–30 minutes

Level

Upper intermediate–Advanced / B2–C1

Language focus

Marketing mix terms

Group formation

Pairs or small groups

Preparation

Make a copy of the grid for each learner.

Copy and cut up the cards, one set for each group.

Lead-in

Ask the learners if they know what the marketing mix is (the combination of activities required to ensure good sales). Write these words on the board: Product, Price, Place (Distribution), Promotion – explain this is the standard marketing mix. Brainstorm several items which could come under these headings, e.g. *brand recognition* (Product), *profit margin* (Price), *retail shops* (Place), *free samples* (Promotion).

Procedure

- Divide the class into pairs or small groups and give a grid to each learner and a set of cards to each pair or group.
- Ask the learners to decide which area of the marketing mix these cards belong to. They should be able to defend their decisions.
- Discuss the answers with the learners (see Introduction).
- Get the learners to write the answers into their grids.
- If learners have items in different places, ask them to explain why. Tell them that there are different ways of looking at these items – the answers only express the traditional or standard way of thinking about these strategies.

Follow-up

Learners choose a specific product and discuss it in terms of the marketing mix.

One-to-one

Discuss the cards and the grid with the learner. Ask the learner to defend the decisions he or she makes regarding the ordering of the cards and discuss the points he or she raises further.

Note

Some marketing experts are now considering adding a fifth 'P' to the mix. It hasn't been decided if it will deal with packaging, process or people. This could be discussed with groups who are particularly interested in marketing.

Vocabulary

accessories additional features or items which can be sold to enhance a product
brand recognition a customer's awareness that a brand exists and can be purchased
consumer durables consumer goods that are not bought regularly and that last a long time, such as cars
credit accounts an arrangement with a company for deferred payment when buying goods (bills are often sent once a month and not when the goods are purchased)
factory outlet shop where a manufacturer sells their products directly to the consumer without a middleman
giveaways free samples given to consumers free of charge as a marketing strategy
generics goods which are sold without a brand name
import tariffs duties (taxes) imposed on imported products by a government
inventory a detailed list of all items in stock
just-in-time delivery having goods delivered just before they are needed, to avoid storage costs
life cycle the amount of time a product is expected to function properly
mailshot the posting of advertising materials to a large number of people at one time
market coverage percentage of a market which the sales cover (also called *market share* and *market penetration*)
mid-range pricing average price for a product, not at the high or low end of the scale
order processing the process of dealing with orders, including entering the details into the computer system, and printing invoices and delivery notes
point of sale a business or place where a product or service can be purchased
product range enhancement adding more products to the group of existing ones
shelf life the length of time a product, especially food, can be kept in a shop before it is too old to sell
sponsorship person or company which pays for advertising for a specific product or event
USP = unique selling proposition (US) what makes a product different from other similar products
USP = unique selling point (UK)
VAT value-added tax, also called **sales tax**, added on to the net price of a product
warehousing storage in a warehouse or similar place for storing goods

The Four Ps

Product	Price	Place	Promotion

The Four Ps

Product	Price	Place	Promotion
product range enhancement	high-end pricing	point of sale	TV commercials
brand recognition	profit margin	factory outlets	free samples
quality control	quantity discount	retail shops	two-for-one sales
research and development	credit accounts	warehousing	newspaper adverts
inventory	payment on delivery	channels of distribution	catalogues
image	price list	transportation	shop displays
guarantees	production costs	internet sales	mailshots, leaflets and fliers
consumer durables	mid-range pricing	chain stores	product endorsement
generics	price war	shopping mall kiosks	promotional campaigns
life cycle	import tariffs	mail order companies	packaging
accessories	VAT	market coverage	giveaways
repairs and support	cash discount	just-in-time delivery	unique selling proposition/point
shelf life	suggested retail price	order processing	sponsorship

A marketing strategy

Type of activity
Creating a marketing strategy

Time
30–45 minutes (including presentations)

Level
Upper intermediate–Advanced / B2–C1

Language focus
Marketing terms

Group formation
Small groups

Preparation
Make a copy of the grid for each group of learners.

Find photos of a product or an actual product to bring to class.

Lead-in
Show the learners a photo of a product or an actual product. This can be something found in the classroom or taken from a magazine or newspaper. Ask them if this is a product they would be interested in buying themselves. Write up the pros and cons of buying the product on the board. Discuss what they would consider to be a good marketing strategy for the product, or talk about the strategy actually used if they know it. Explain that they are now going to create a marketing strategy for a product.

Activity 6.1 could also be used as a lead-in to this activity.

Procedure
- Divide the class into small groups and give each group a copy of the grid.
- Let them choose a product and then fill in the right-hand column of the grid to design a marketing strategy.
- Depending on the amount of time available, the last three points in the grid can be included or left out. (The learners will need extra paper to do these. They could also be done as homework and presented in the next lesson.)
- When the groups have finished, they present their strategy to the others.
- Learners should be encouraged to explain why they chose the ideas they did and be able to defend their decisions.

Follow-up
This activity could be followed up with a SWOT analysis. When the groups have finished their presentations, the class works together on a SWOT analysis of the ideas and of the product itself. The following grid can be drawn on the board or put on an OHP. Then the class can brainstorm ideas to fit into the categories of the grid.

Strengths	**Weaknesses**
Opportunities	**Threats**

One-to-one
Discuss the strategy with the learner. This is especially appropriate for learners in the fields of marketing or advertising. If possible, a real product from the learner's company should be chosen to make the activity more meaningful.

Note
Learners will need some monitoring as well as help with the language. The marketing mix cards can be given to the groups to help them with some of the language whether or not they did Activity 6.1.

Vocabulary
to launch to put a product on the market and begin to advertise and sell it
radio commercial an advertisement on the radio
SWOT analysis a marketing technique which deals with strengths, weaknesses, opportunities and threats, usually discussed when planning or launching a new product
target group the group of consumers the product is aimed at

Marketing strategy

Choose a product.	
Decide which target group the product should appeal to.	
Choose a new name for the product.	
Decide where and when to launch the product.	
Decide on the USPs (unique selling propositions) for the product. Think of at least three points.	
Determine the price.	
Decide on the distribution channels.	
Decide where the product will be sold.	
Plan a promotional campaign. Keep the AIDA formula in mind: **A**ttention: create awareness of the product **I**nterest: appeal to the customer and create confidence in the product **D**esire: create a feeling of need for the product **A**ction: trigger the customer's actual buying of the product	
Create an interesting design for the package. (optional)	
Write a 30-second radio commercial. (optional)	
Design an advertisement for a magazine or newspaper. (optional)	

Advertising

Type of activity

Ordering

Creating an advertisement

Time

30–45 minutes (including several presentations)

Level

Upper intermediate–Advanced / B2–C1

Language focus

Language to describe products; language of persuasion

Group formation

Pairs or small groups

Preparation

If possible, find adverts for products in English (in magazines, newspapers or on the internet).

Make a copy of the complete grid for each person in the class.

Copy and cut up a set of the cards for each group of learners.

Lead-in

Show the learners several advertisements in English which contain phrases dealing with physical, emotional and intellectual language, using ideas from the grid. Ask the learners to look at the language (slogans and product descriptions) and write down the phrases which they find convincing or important for selling the product.

If you don't have any advertisements, brainstorm the different types of language, using ideas from the grid.

Explain that copywriters use different techniques to get the attention of consumers.

Procedure

- Write the words *physical*, *emotional* and *intellectual* on the board. Ask learners what these words mean to them. Then show them a card for each of these categories and ask them where they think they belong.
- Put the learners into pairs or small groups and give each group a set of cards.
- Tell them to sort the cards into the three categories. They should be able to defend their decisions. As some of the cards can fit into more than one category, any convincing argument is acceptable.
- Discuss the answers with the learners (see Introduction). Encourage them to think of other phrases and write them into the grid.
- Ask each group to choose a product and think of phrases of their own that would be suitable for an advertisement for it. Learners should think about the language they need and which ideas they can include. They can also discuss how things might be different for a magazine ad, a TV commercial or a radio commercial and give reasons.
- When the groups have finished, they present their ideas to the others.

Follow-up

This activity can be followed up with the writing of a TV or radio commercial using the various types of language which have been taught. The entire campaign can then be presented to the class. If one product is chosen by the class, each group could be instructed to pitch their advertisement, and the class can then decide which one they would choose if they were the client.

If they have already written a radio commercial for Activity 6.2, the learners can look at it again from the point of view of this new language input. Alternatively, they could choose a different medium and write a new advertisement.

One-to-one

The learner can work with the teacher to discuss the different types of language and complete the grid.

Note

The aim of the activity is not for the learners to write perfect adverts but rather to make them aware of the type of language commonly used and to give them a chance to tap into their creativity. For those learners who work in marketing or advertising, this exercise could be particularly helpful, as they can also use the ideas and transfer them to their mother tongue.

Vocabulary

ad/advert/advertisement a notice which gives information about a product and whose purpose is to make the product known and persuade the consumer to buy it. (As abbreviations, **ad** is more common in the US, **advert** is more common in the UK.)
to bridge the gap to connect two items or things
commercial an advertisement for television or radio
copywriter a person responsible for writing the text of advertisements
to join the ranks become part of a group of people
slogan a phrase or words which are easy to remember, used in publicity for a product, service or company
well-being the state of feeling healthy

Advertising styles

Physical	Emotional	Intellectual

Cards

Physical	Emotional	Intellectual
Feel the difference!	Your satisfaction is our goal.	Thinking people buy our products.
Get the taste of it!	Enjoy the feeling of having a dream come true.	Enjoy the knowledge that you have made a wise choice.
Just jump in and try it!	Would you also like to experience the feeling of success?	Make use of our state-of-the-art technology.
Forget about theory – put yourself in our hands for a practical approach.	Come to the company which puts your well-being first.	Innovation and perfection are the goals we strive for.
Our goal is to get you where you want to go.	Experience customer service from the caring company.	The informed consumer is our target group.
Sit back and relax, knowing that you have put your money to work for you.	Our mission is to ensure a future for your grandchildren through our commitment to the environment.	Our expertise in the field is unchallenged.
Help us bridge the gap between products and service.	Hope is the best resource we can imagine.	We are looking for customers who can think for themselves and make wise decisions.
Join the ranks of hands-on users.	Are you looking for a product which fits your lifestyle and expresses who you really are?	Our products combine intelligent solutions and reliability.
Get in touch with us if you have any questions about our products or services.	Enjoy the comfort of being one of our valued customers.	Heightened awareness of our products has led to worldwide recognition and praise.

Terms used in balance sheets

Type of activity
Matching

Time
30 minutes

Level
Intermediate–Upper intermediate / B1–B2

Language focus
Balance sheet terms

Group formation
Groups of three

Preparation
Copy the grid with the definitions, one for each learner.

Copy and cut up the sheet with the cards, one set for each learner. Keep the cards in their three separate categories.

Lead-in
Ask learners if they have worked with balance sheets. Brainstorm the words they know. Write some of these on the board and discuss them.

Procedure
- Divide the class into three groups. In large classes, these groups can be subdivided into smaller groups.
- Give each of the three groups the grid with the definitions and a set of cards which applies to one of the three areas on the grid (Fixed assets, Current assets or Creditors). Get the learners to match the financial terms to the definitions for that area and write the terms in the grid.
- When they have finished with one section, they can exchange cards with the other groups and do the next section, then change again to do the last section.
- Discuss answers with the learners (see Introduction) and check that they have written the correct terms next to the appropriate definitions.

One-to-one
The teacher and the learner do the matching together.

Vocabulary
accrued recorded over a period of time
cash in hand the amount of money in the form of cash that a company has after it has paid all its costs
deferred put off to a later date
intangible something which has no physical presence and is not visible
nominal value the stated value of a share when it is issued
tangible something which has a physical presence and is visible

Balance sheet terms

Fixed assets	**things belonging to a company which have value**
	something that has no physical presence, but has value (including patents, trademarks and brands)
	expenses that go into creating products
	official documents giving a company the sole right to make or sell a particular product or process
	a symbol which is used by a company for a product or process and is protected by law
	the total market value of a company minus the net value of its tangible assets
	things owned by a person or company which actually exist and are of value to the owner
	a manufacturing factory and its equipment as well as the place of business and the necessary business tools and machines
	articles attached to or fixed in place in a building or factory
Current assets	**assets used by a company in its ordinary work**
	components and finished goods which are stockpiled by a company and have not yet been sold, and work in progress
	substances held by the manufacturer for use in the production process
	partially-manufactured products at various stages of completion
	money that is currently owed to a company by its customers
	money that a company has already paid to its suppliers in advance of work done
	money invested in securities for less than one year
	investments such as stocks and shares which cannot be readily converted into cash
	assets such as money in the bank or cash in hand
Creditors	**other companies or people to whom a company owes money**
	amounts of money owed by a business to its suppliers or employees
	bills which the company has received and not yet paid
	the part of a long-term loan which will need to be paid within the next 12 months
	amount of tax which will have to be paid in the future
	money owed which must be paid back within the next twelve months
	the amount owed to a bank and payable on demand
	a company's capital which is owned by its shareholders
	the nominal value of the shares held by the shareholders

Cards

Fixed assets	**Current assets**	**Creditors**
intangible assets	*stock*	*trade creditors*
development costs	*raw materials*	*accrued expenses*
patents	*work in progress*	*current portion of long-term debt*
trademark	*trade debtors*	*deferred corporation tax*
goodwill	*prepaid expenses*	*short-term debt*
tangible assets	*short-term investments*	*overdraft*
plant and machinery	*long-term investments*	*shareholders' funds*
fixtures and fittings	*cash at bank and in hand*	*share capital*

Key

Fixed assets	**things belonging to a company which have value**
intangible assets	something that has no physical presence, but has value (including patents, trademarks and brands)
development costs	expenses that go into creating products
patents	official documents giving a company the sole right to make or sell a particular product or process
trademark	a symbol protected by law and used by a company for a product or process
goodwill	the total market value of a company minus the net value of its tangible assets
tangible assets	things owned by a person or company which actually exist and are of value to the owner
plant and machinery	a manufacturing factory and its equipment as well as the place of business and the necessary business tools and machines
fixtures and fittings	articles attached to or fixed in place in a building or factory
Current assets	**assets used by a company in its ordinary work**
stock	components and finished goods which are stockpiled by a company and have not yet been sold, and work in progress
raw materials	substances held by the manufacturer for use in the production process
work in progress	partially-manufactured products at various stages of completion
trade debtors	money that is currently owed to a company by its customers
prepaid expenses	money that a company has already paid to its suppliers in advance of work done
short-term investments	money invested in securities for less than one year
long-term investments	investments such as stocks and shares which cannot be readily converted into cash
cash at bank and in hand	assets such as money in the bank or cash in hand
Creditors	**other companies or people to whom a company owes money**
trade creditors	amounts of money owed by a business to its suppliers or employees
accrued expenses	bills which the company has received and not yet paid
current portion of long-term debt	the part of a long-term loan which will need to be paid within the next 12 months
deferred corporation tax	amount of tax which will have to be paid in the future
short-term debt	money owed which must be paid back within the next twelve months
overdraft	the amount owed to a bank and payable on demand
shareholders' funds	a company's capital which is owned by its shareholders
share capital	the nominal value of the shares held by the shareholders

The balance sheet

Type of activity

Information gap

Time

15 minutes

Level

Intermediate–Upper intermediate / B1–B2

Language focus

Balance sheet terms; numbers

Group formation

Pairs

Preparation

Copy sheet A for half the class and sheet B for the other half.

Lead-in

Ask learners if they have worked with balance sheets. Brainstorm the words they know. Write some of these on the board and discuss them.

For some classes, it might be a good idea to revise large numbers and how they are said.

Activity 7.1 could also be used as a lead-in to this activity.

Procedure

- Divide the class into pairs and give one person sheet A and the other person sheet B.
- Tell them to fill in the missing information on their sheets by asking their partner for it.
- Get the partners to compare their sheets to make sure that they wrote everything correctly.
- Discuss the answers with the learners (see Introduction).

Follow-up

If learners have actual balance sheets from their companies, these can be looked at and compared with the practice sheets.

One-to-one

The teacher and the learner do the activity together.

Note

This is an example of a UK balance sheet. US balance sheets may differ

Pre-teach or elicit questions that the learners will find useful, e.g. *What's the figure for …? How much was spent on …? What cost …?*

There is a euro symbol in the balance sheet, but other currencies can be substituted for this if the teacher wishes.

Balance sheet A

Company ABC		
At December 31	2005	2004
	€	€
	millions	millions
Fixed assets		
Intangible assets		
________	3,050	2,569
Patents, licences and trademarks	________	1,205
Goodwill	250	275
	4,750	4,049
Tangible assets		
________	24,450	22,350
Plant and machinery, technical equipment	25,890	________
Fixtures, fittings, tools and equipment	11,243	10,410
	61,583	54,520
	66,333	58,569
Current assets		
Stock		
Raw materials	________	2,983
Work in progress	4,531	5,210
Finished goods	2,579	________
	10,532	11,162
Trade debtors	9,875	11,643
________	2,886	3,421
Short-term investments	________	10,984
Long-term investments	13,980	13,980
Other assets	72,659	________
Cash at bank and in hand	9,887	12,117
	126,711	131,730
Creditors: amounts falling due within one year		
Trade creditors	20,723	29,332
________	9,452	8,987
Current portion of long-term debt	12,979	9,989
Deferred corporation tax	11,853	________
Short-term debt	92,321	89,345
Overdraft	2,345	2,976
	149,673	150,288
Net current liabilities/assets	–22,962	–18,558
Total assets less current liabilities	43,371	40,011
Creditors: amounts falling due after one year	________	16,909
Net assets	23,000	23,102
Shareholders' funds		
Share capital	13,256	13,256
Other capital	________	9,846
	23,000	23,102

Balance sheet B

Company ABC		
At December 31	2005	2004
	€	€
	millions	millions
Fixed assets		
Intangible assets		
Development costs	3,050	2,569
Patents, licences and trademarks	1,450	______
______	250	275
	4,750	4,049
Tangible assets		
Land and buildings	24,450	22,350
Plant and machinery, technical equipment	25,890	21,760
Fixtures, fittings, tools and equipment	______	10,410
	61,583	54,520
	66,333	58,569
Current assets		
Stock		
Raw materials	3,422	______
______	4,531	5,210
Finished goods	2,579	2,969
	10,532	11,162
Trade debtors	______	11,643
Prepaid expenses	2,886	3,421
Short-term investments	6,892	10,984
______	13,980	13,980
Other assets	72,659	68,423
Cash at bank and in hand	9,887	______
	126,711	131,730
Creditors: amounts falling due within one year		
______	20,723	29,332
Accrued expenses	9,452	8,987
Current portion of long-term debt	______	9,989
Deferred corporation tax	11,853	9,659
Short-term debt	92,321	89,345
Overdraft	2,345	______
	149,673	150,288
Net current liabilities/assets	-22,962	-18,558
Total assets less current liabilities	43,371	______
Creditors: amounts falling due after one year	20,371	16,909
Net assets	23,000	23,102
Shareholders' funds		
______	13,256	______
Other capital	9,744	9,846
	23,000	23,102

Key

Company ABC

At December 31	2005	2004
	€	€
	millions	millions
Fixed assets		
Intangible assets		
Development costs	3,050	2,569
Patents, licences and trademarks	1,450	1,205
Goodwill	250	275
	4,750	4,049
Tangible assets		
Land and buildings	24,450	22,350
Plant and machinery, technical equipment	25,890	21,760
Fixtures, fittings, tools and equipment	11,243	10,410
	61,583	54,520
	66,333	58,569
Current assets		
Stock		
Raw materials	3,422	2,983
Work in progress	4,531	5,210
Finished goods	2,579	2,969
	10,532	11,162
Trade debtors	9,875	11,643
Prepaid expenses	2,886	3,421
Short-term investments	6,892	10,984
Long-term investments	13,980	13,980
Other assets	72,659	68,423
Cash at bank and in hand	9,887	12,117
	126,711	131,730
Creditors: amounts falling due within one year		
Trade creditors	20,723	29,332
Accrued expenses	9,452	8,987
Current portion of long-term debt	12,979	9,989
Deferred corporation tax	11,853	9,659
Short-term debt	92,321	89,345
Overdraft	2,345	2,976
	149,673	150,288
Net current liabilities/assets	-22,962	-18,558
Total assets less current liabilities	43,371	40,011
Creditors: amounts falling due after one year	20,371	16,909
Net assets	23,000	23,102
Shareholders' funds		
Share capital	13,256	13,256
Other capital	9,744	9,846
	23,000	23,102

Financial news

Type of activity
Correct the mistakes

Time
20–30 minutes

Level
Intermediate–Upper intermediate / B1–B2

Language focus
Balance sheets and financial reports

Language of change *(increase, decrease, remain stable …)*

Group formation
Pairs

Preparation
Copy the balance sheet key from Activity 7.2, one for each learner. (If Activity 7.2 was done, ask the learners to bring their copy to class.)

Copy the news sheet, one for each learner and fold it along the dotted line above the key.

Lead-in
Ask learners if they have worked with balance sheets. Brainstorm the words they know. Write some of these on the board and discuss them.

For some classes, it might be a good idea to revise large numbers and how they are said. Check the learners know the appropriate terms to show change, e.g. *increase, decrease.*

Activity 7.1 and 7.2 could also be used as lead-ins to this activity.

Procedure
- Divide the class into pairs and give each pair the news sheet. Tell them to make sure that it is folded where indicated. Let them read the newspaper report and then discuss it.
- Give out the balance sheet (the key from Activity 7.2) and tell the learners that this is the balance sheet that the report is about but that there are several mistakes in the report.
- Tell the learners to work together to find the mistakes in the report.
- The learners rewrite the report correctly, based on the information they have on their balance sheets.
- Discuss the answers with the learners (see Introduction).

Follow-up
Ask learners to bring balance sheets from their companies to class if possible. They could discuss these briefly and write a report on one of them, using the financial report as a model.

Advanced learners who have access to balance sheets in English can discuss the differences in vocabulary used and how the balance sheets are structured.

One-to-one
The teacher and the learner read and discuss the financial report together. The learner can then rewrite the report as homework. Alternatively, the learner could write a report about his or her own company based on actual figures if those are available.

News

Looking back at the years 2004–2005, we can see that the company was going through some interesting changes at the time. For example, the net assets increased slightly. In addition, the figure of the work in progress was at €4,531,000 in 2004 and rose to €5,210,000 in 2005.

The other areas of the balance sheet show an increase in intangible assets overall. Each of the positions increased in 2005. There was also an increase in finished goods. Long-term investments remained stable but the amounts owed by trade debtors rose by about 2,000,000 from 2004 to 2005.

Looking at creditors, the short-term debt went up by almost 30,000,000 in 2005. The amounts owed to trade creditors fell in 2005, as did the deferred corporation tax. The current portion of long-term debt showed a decrease in 2005 but the overdraft indicated an increase. Accrued expenses fell from 2004 to 2005.

In addition, the share capital and the other capital under the heading of shareholders' funds showed little change.

Fold here --

Key (suggested answer)

Looking back at the years 2004–2005, we can see that the company was going through some interesting changes at the time. For example, the net assets **decreased** slightly. In addition, the figure of the work in progress was at **€4,531,000 in 2005, falling from €5,210,000 in 2004**.

The other areas of the balance sheet show an increase in intangible assets overall. **Two out of the three** positions increased in 2005. There was, **however, a decrease** in finished goods. Long-term investments remained stable but the amounts owed by trade debtors **fell** by about 2,000,000 from 2004 to 2005.

Looking at creditors, the short-term debt went up by almost **3,000,000** in 2005. The amounts owed to trade creditors fell in 2005, **but the deferred corporation tax increased**. The current portion of long-term debt showed **an increase** in 2005 but the overdraft indicated **a decrease**. Accrued expenses **rose** from 2004 to 2005.

In addition, the share capital and the other capital under the heading of shareholders' funds showed little change.

Finance triangle

Type of activity
Matching

Time
15 minutes

Level
Intermediate–Upper intermediate / B1–B2

Language focus
Terms used in balance sheets and financial reports

Group formation
Groups of three

Preparation
Copy and cut up the vocabulary triangle grid, sheets A, B and C, for each group of learners.

Lead-in
Ask learners if they have worked with balance sheets. Brainstorm the words they know. Write some of these on the board and discuss them.

Activity 7.1 could also be used as a lead-in to this activity.

Procedure
- Divide the class into three groups. In large classes, these groups can be subdivided into smaller groups.
- Give each learner in a group one of the sheets of the vocabulary triangle (A, B or C).
- Tell them that the terms used in balance sheets and financial reports are in the left-hand column and the definitions are in the right-hand column. The terms and definitions on their sheet match with ones on the sheets which the other learners have. They must work together to match the terms with the definitions.
- Learner A begins by reading the term in the top left-hand corner. B and C look for the definition on the right-hand side of their page and when someone has found it, he or she reads it aloud. Then he or she reads the term directly opposite (on the same line) to the other two learners, who look for the definition and read the term opposite, and so on. The last word to be read is the word in the top right-hand corner of sheet A.

One-to-one
The learner can work with one of the sheets, while the teacher uses the other two. A strong learner could have two of the sheets while the teacher has one.

Note
All the terms and definitions are in the key for Activity 7.1.

Finance triangle

A

trade creditors	money invested in securities for less than one year
trademark	bills which the company has received and not yet paid
prepaid expenses	expenses that go into creating products
shareholders' funds	official documents giving a company the sole right to make or sell a particular product or process
deferred corporation tax	partially-manufactured products at various stages of completion
fixtures and fittings	things owned by a person or company which actually exist and are of value to the owner
short-term debt	substances held by the manufacturer for use in the production process
goodwill	components and finished goods which are stockpiled by the company and have not yet been sold, and work in progress

B

current portion of long-term debt	the nominal value of the shares held by the shareholders
patents	the total market value of a company minus the net value of the tangible assets
short-term investments	investments such as stocks and shares which cannot be readily converted into cash
cash at bank and in hand	the amount owed to a bank and payable on demand
accrued expenses	a company's capital which is owned by its shareholders
work in progress	money that is currently owed to a company by its customers
intangible assets	a manufacturing factory and its equipment as well as the place of business and the necessary business tools and machines
development costs	money owed which must be paid back within the next twelve months

C

trade debtors	assets such as money in the bank or cash in hand
long-term investments	money that a company has already paid to its suppliers in advance of work done
plant and machinery	amounts of money owed by a business to its suppliers or employees
overdraft	the part of a long-term loan which will need to be paid within the next 12 months
stock	something that has no physical presence but has value (including patents, trademarks and brands)
tangible assets	a symbol protected by law and used by a company for a product or process
raw materials	amount of tax which will have to be paid in the future
share capital	articles attached to or fixed in place in a building or factory

Find someone who knows ...

Type of activity
Find someone who ...

Time
10–15 minutes

Level
Intermediate / B1

Language focus
Common business terms for marketing and finance

Group formation
Whole class

Preparation
Copy and cut up the sheet with the cards.

Lead-in
Discuss how much learners are involved in marketing or finance, or what they know about these areas.

If learners are not familiar with these terms, give the cards out (one or two for each learner) and tell them to find the meaning of their word(s) in a business dictionary. Then collect and shuffle the cards before doing the activity.

Procedure
- Depending on the number of learners, give each person in the class one or two cards.
- Elicit or revise the phrases *Do you know what 'x' is?* and *Do you know what 'x' means?*
- Tell the learners to find out what the meanings of the terms are by asking other learners in the class.
- Set a time limit for learners to do the activity, depending on the number in the class.
- Discuss the answers with the learners (see Introduction). Note that the definitions for all the terms used are in the key for Activity 8.2.

Follow-up
The terms in this activity can be reviewed by putting the class into groups and getting each group to choose seven to ten of the words. Each learner takes a word and has to describe it to his or her own team, who have to say what the word means. Set a time limit of 45 seconds for the description. The team gets a point for each word which was defined correctly.

In monolingual classes and where appropriate, groups can find the translations in their mother tongue and do the activity by using the translation of the term.

Put the class into pairs and get them to write dialogues using as many of the words as possible.

One-to-one
The learner and the teacher look through the terms and discuss them together. The teacher can begin by asking the learner how many of the terms he or she has heard of and then discuss the relevance of them to the particular field the learner works in.

Cards

Find someone who knows what this means: **AIDA**	Find someone who knows what this means: **USP**	Find someone who knows what this means: **loss leader**
Find someone who knows what this means: **cash cow**	Find someone who knows what this means: **gross margin**	Find someone who knows what this means: **net profit**
Find someone who knows what this means: **break-even point**	Find someone who knows what this means: **budget**	Find someone who knows what this means: **expenditure**
Find someone who knows what this means: **variable costs**	Find someone who knows what this means: **market leader**	Find someone who knows what this means: **niche market**
Find someone who knows what this means: **target group**	Find someone who knows what this means: **product launch**	Find someone who knows what this means: **focus group**
Find someone who knows what this means: **turnover**	Find someone who knows what this means: **the 4 Ps**	Find someone who knows what this means: **brand awareness**
Find someone who knows what this means: **bankruptcy**	Find someone who knows what this means: **creditors**	Find someone who knows what this means: **collateral**

Definitions

Type of activity
Defining terms + matching

Time
20 minutes

Level
Intermediate / B1

Language focus
Common business terms for marketing and finance

Group formation
Pairs or small groups

Preparation
Copy the worksheet (one for each learner).

If the learners don't know the majority of the terms for these definitions, copy the cards from Activity 8.1 and cut them up, one set of cards for each group of learners.

Lead-in
Discuss how much learners are involved in marketing or finance, or what they know about these areas.

Activity 8.1 could also be used as a lead-in to this activity.

Procedure
- Divide the class into pairs or small groups.
- If learners know the majority of the terms, get them to discuss each definition and write the appropriate term next to it. Otherwise, give out the cards from Activity 8.1 and tell them to match them with the definitions. Encourage them to do the ones they feel they know first, to narrow the choices for the remaining definitions.
- The learners should also write M (for marketing) or F (for finance) in the brackets next to each term, depending on which area it is most closely related to.
- They can join another group when they have done all the ones they know and help each other to complete the task.
- Discuss the answers with the learners (see Introduction).

One to one
The learner either tries to think of the correct term for each definition or uses the cards from Activity 8.1 and matches them with the terms.

Follow-up
The terms in this activity can be reviewed by getting the learners to read the definitions to each other and asking for the correct term.

Definitions

1 This means *attention, interest, desire* and *action*. This is a strategy used to sell products. ____________________ ( )

2 This refers to selling a product at a loss to get customers into the shop. The shop owner then hopes that they will buy other products they hadn't planned to buy. ____________________ ( )

3 This is the difference between the cost of manufacturing a product and how much it is sold for. ____________________ ( )

4 This occurs when sales are equal to costs. ____________________ ( )

5 This refers to features of your product which other products do not have. ____________________ ( )

6 This is a specific amount of money spent. ____________________ ( )

7 This refers to a company or product with the largest market share. ____________________ ( )

8 This refers to the money that is left over after all expenses have been deducted. ____________________ ( )

9 This is a small speciality market with little competition in it. ____________________ ( )

10 This is a plan for spending and income. ____________________ ( )

11 This is a group of people who come together informally to discuss their reactions to a product. ____________________ ( )

12 This refers to the money needed to produce a product, which increases according to the number of products produced. ____________________ ( )

13 This refers to putting a new product on the market. ____________________ ( )

14 This is the total amount of sales of goods or services of a company. ____________________ ( )

15 This refers to the product, the price of the product, the place it is distributed and sold, and its promotion. These are the factors considered in the marketing campaign. ____________________ ( )

16 This term indicates how well known a particular brand is. ____________________ ( )

17 This occurs when a company is no longer able to pay its debts. ____________________ ( )

18 This is a type of security required in order to get a loan. ____________________ ( )

19 This is a product which needs little advertising and always sells well. This can be due to the demand for the type of product or the brand awareness. ____________________ ( )

20 These are the people a company or person owes money to. ____________________ ( )

21 This refers to the group of people which a product is aimed at. ____________________ ( )

Key

1 This means *attention, interest, desire* and *action*. This is a strategy used to sell products. **AIDA (M)**

2 This refers to selling a product at a loss to get customers into the shop. The shop owner then hopes that they will buy other products they hadn't planned to buy. **loss leader (M)**

3 This is the difference between the cost of manufacturing a product and how much it is sold for. **gross margin (F)**

4 This occurs when sales are equal to costs. **break-even point (F)**

5 This refers to features of your product which other products do not have. **USP (M)**

6 This is a specific amount of money spent. **expenditure (F)**

7 This refers to a company or product with the largest market share. **market leader (M)**

8 This refers to the money that is left over after all expenses have been deducted. **net profit (F)**

9 This is a small speciality market with little competition in it. **niche market (M)**

10 This is a plan for spending and income. **budget (F)**

11 This is a group of people who come together informally to discuss their reactions to a product. **focus group (M)**

12 This refers to the money needed to produce a product, which increases according to the number of products produced. **variable costs (F)**

13 This refers to putting a new product on the market. **product launch (M)**

14 This is the total amount of sales of goods or services of a company. **turnover (F)**

15 This refers to the product, the price of the product, the place it is distributed and sold, and its promotion. These are the factors considered in the marketing campaign. **the 4 Ps (M)**

16 This term indicates how well known a particular brand is. **brand awareness (M)**

17 This occurs when a company is no longer able to pay its debts. **bankruptcy (F)**

18 This is a type of security required in order to get a loan. **collateral (F)**

19 This is a product which needs little advertising and always sells well. This can be due to the demand for the type of product or the brand awareness. **cash cow (M)**

20 These are the people a company or person owes money to. **creditors (F)**

21 This refers to the group of people which a product is aimed at. **target group (M)**

The new canteen

Type of activity
Holding a meeting

Time
60 minutes (+10–15 minutes for follow-up discussions)

Level
Upper intermediate–Advanced / B2–C1

Language focus
Language of meetings, e.g. asking for and giving opinions

Group formation
Groups of four to six (for smaller groups, the trade union representative and head of maintenance could be omitted)

Preparation
Copy the information sheet for each learner.

Copy one role card for each learner in the group.

Lead-in
Ask the learners what types of meetings they attend. Elicit the different functions of language in a meeting (opening a meeting, asking for and giving opinions, expressing agreement and disagreement, making suggestions, interrupting someone, getting back to the topic, calling for a vote and closing a meeting).

Write the functions on the board as the learners suggest them and elicit a phrase for each category.

Put the learners into small groups to work together to find more phrases for these categories. Discuss the phrases they have found with the class.

Procedure
- Put the learners into groups of six (or fewer, omitting the trade union representative and head of maintenance) and give out the information sheet. In large classes, you could have groups of seven, with one learner being a 'secretary' who takes notes.
- Give the learners time to read the information and become familiar with the situation.
- Give out the role cards. Make sure that a strong learner takes on the role of managing director.
- Hold the meeting.
- Discuss the outcome with the learners.
- If a secretary was appointed, he or she can report on the results, and his or her notes can be used to write up the minutes of the meeting.

Note
Phrases for the categories in Lead-in can include:

Opening a meeting: *I would like to open this meeting. I declare this meeting open. (in formal meetings)*

Asking for opinions: *What do you think about this? Let's hear from …*

Giving opinions: *I think … I believe … In my opinion … From my point of view …*

Expressing agreement: *Fine with me. I agree. That's a good idea. OK.*

Expressing disagreement: *Yes, but … I don't agree. I don't think that will work.*

Making suggestions: *I propose that we … I would like to suggest that …*

Interrupting someone: *Sorry to interrupt, but … Can I just say something about …?*

Getting back to the topic: *If we could continue to discuss … I think we are off the point. Can we come back to …?*

Calling for a vote: *Can we put this to the vote? All in favour? Anyone against? Any abstentions?*

Closing the meeting: *I declare this meeting closed. This meeting is now closed. (in formal meetings)*

Vocabulary
to cash in to use a voucher instead of money
corporate image how a company wants to be seen by the public
desertification the transformation of farm land to desert caused by mismanagement of land and resources
fair trade an agreement to enforce price supports for commodities, especially those bought from developing countries
food voucher a written authorization which allows people to buy meals in restaurants which are subsidized by their companies
hearty substantial, providing abundant nourishment
middlemen people who buy from the producer and sell to the consumer
mission statement a written policy stating the goals and priorities of an organization
organic foods food grown without the use of chemicals
on the premises in a company's buildings or on its land
track record the reputation of a person or company, which can be easily seen or found out about
subsidized paid for in part by an organization
unqualified support complete support

Information

The company

Business: import
Goods: fair trade products from developing countries
Size: medium but growing
Number of employees at main office: 250
Location: a capital city in Europe
Reason for meeting: Your company has been growing due to the widespread interest in fair trade products, and you have recently hired a number of new employees. Part of your corporate image is to treat employees fairly and provide them with as many services and benefits as possible while maintaining your profit margins.
Until now, employees have received food vouchers, which they could cash in at local restaurants or shops near the office. Management has recently been thinking about having a canteen on the premises and has therefore contacted several different companies about in-house catering services.
The priorities for the management board include providing healthy food at a fair price and in keeping with the general corporate image of the company. The canteen would be subsidized by the company to keep the prices reasonable for the employees. It would have to be non-smoking to be in line with your office policy of no smoking in the workplace.
A meeting has been called to decide if a canteen should be established and to discuss the various proposals put forward by different catering companies.

Catering companies

The Farmers' Market a small cooperative catering company which buys food directly from local farmers. They provide hearty meals and the food is guaranteed to be fresh. As they buy from the farmers in the area, their menus are based on food which is in season. They have been in business for the past 15 years.
Price range: medium
Variety: limited

The farmers' market

The Organic Store *a new company which started up several months ago and has been looking for opportunities to sell their goods and services. They have several chefs who create interesting and tasty menus using only organic foods. They buy them from local farmers as well as from abroad. They also buy through middlemen from developing markets.*
Price range: medium to high
Variety: large selection

The organic store

Fair Trade Catering a company which is two years old and uses only fair trade products. They have a track record of helping developing countries by buying directly from farmers. They also support projects such as building schools, providing clean water and working against the desertification affecting many areas of Africa. Due to the high price of particular fair trade items such as chocolate and coffee, some of their prices are quite high. They have also had problems lately with one of their chefs and are looking for a new one at the moment.
Price range: high
Variety: large selection

F
Fair trade catering

Roles

Managing director
Your job is to run the meeting.
As the canteen was your idea, you definitely want to open one.
You have tasted the food from all the catering companies and think that the organic food tastes the best. However, you have heard that at least half of the products they use are bought through middlemen and are not fair trade products. You want to hear what the others in your company say before you give them this information.
You are not sure about recommending the Organic Store too strongly. It could damage the corporate image of the company if word about it got out and it had your unqualified support.
Your second choice would be the Farmer's Market, although you think that many employees would be bored with the food after several months.

Finance director
You are not sure that the idea of a canteen is a good one as it will probably cost the company too much money. The subsidized food vouchers have worked very well and the local restaurants and shops are also happy with the arrangement. If the decision is made to have a canteen on the premises, you will be in charge of making sure that the prices are kept down. You are responsible for making sure that the company makes a profit and you don't really see the benefits of subsidizing an expensive canteen.

Human resources director
You think a canteen is a benefit for your employees and you like the idea of organic food. You generally try to eat healthy food and find it difficult to find organic food near the company. As part of your job is to look after the well-being of the employees, you are in favour of them being able to get good food without leaving the building.

Public relations director
Your job is to make sure that the image of the company stays consistent with its mission statement. You are really beginning to make a name for yourselves as the leading fair trade company in the area and you are totally against anything that would hurt that image. Therefore, the only catering company which you would consider is the one which buys fair trade products. You also think that having such a catering company on your premises could be used to promote your image and would lead to greater awareness of the company as well as higher profits in the long run.

Trade union representative
You like the idea of a canteen on the premises. Some of the employees have complained about going out in bad weather. Your only concern is that the food may be more expensive and that the lunch hours may be shortened. You prefer simple food so if you have to vote for one catering company, it will be the Farmers' Market.

Head of maintenance
You don't like the idea at all of having a canteen on the premises. Your staff have enough to do without cleaning up food as well. You also like to get out at lunchtime and want to be able to go to a local place where you can enjoy a cigarette and eat what you like. Try to block the idea completely.

Dealing with colleagues

Type of activity
Matching

Time
10–15 minutes

Level
Intermediate / B1

Language focus
Language of bargaining, reaching agreement, internal negotiations

Group formation
Pairs

Preparation
Copy and cut up the cards, one set per pair.

Lead-in
Ask learners if they have participated in any kind of negotiation in their companies. For learners who have not yet had on-the-job experience, remind them that negotiations are also a form of bargaining and can occur in their private lives as well. Elicit examples from learners. If they are experienced negotiators, ask them to describe what types of negotiations they have. If they are not, ask them to think of situations such as trying to get a salary rise or change their job descriptions, or something from their private lives such as buying a car or flat. Brainstorm phrases which they might need. Stress the fact that, especially with internal negotiations, it is important to come to an agreement which benefits both sides.

Procedure
- Divide the class into pairs and give out a set of cards to each pair.
- Tell the learners to match the sentence halves, using grammatical and lexical clues as well as thinking about the meaning of the completed phrase.
- Discuss the answers with the learners (see Introduction).

Follow-up
Ask the pairs to come up with their own phrases and write them down. They can also write them as half sentences on cards and give them to the next group to put together. (They should be checked by the teacher before being passed on to another group.)

One-to-one
The learner works with the cards and discusses the phrases with the teacher.

Vocabulary
action plan a strategy to realize an idea
to bear in mind not to forget
concerns worries
to devise to create
generation (of a product) a newer and more modern version
to implement to put into practice
operative important
option possibility
proposal suggestion
to tackle a problem a way to deal with a difficult situation and to find a solution for it
vital extremely important
to weigh up to consider carefully

Cards

If we agree with your proposal,	can you give us more time to implement the changes?
I see your point,	but I feel that we need to look at the issue from a different point of view.
Would you be	willing to discuss an alternative plan?
Can we set up another meeting	to talk through the ideas?
What would you	think about devising a new action plan?
Can we take some	time to discuss our options?
It seems to me that the operative phrase	here is *customer satisfaction*.
Do you see a way to	find a solution which will make us both happy?
How would you suggest	tackling this problem?
Let's take a look at the	problem from a different perspective.
If you could tell me what your concerns are, we	could begin to look for a satisfactory solution.
I think it is also vital to	weigh up the advantages and disadvantages of the development process.
You need to understand that this	really matters to the future of the company.
We need to bear in mind that	our competitors are already working on the next generation of the product.

10.2 Negotiations

Departmental heads

Type of activity
Role play

Time
45–60 minutes

Level
Upper-intermediate–Advanced / B2–C1

Language focus
Language of negotiations

Group formation
Groups of four

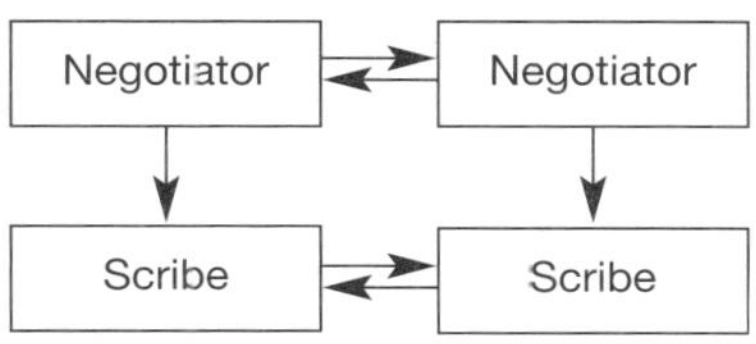

Preparation
Copy the information sheet for each learner.

Copy the role cards one role for half of the learners, the other role for the other half.

Lead-in
Ask the learners about their negotiating experiences and remind them that negotiations are also a form of bargaining and can occur in their private lives as well. Elicit examples from the learners. Discuss the situations they come up with and ask what went well and where problems arose.

Activity 10.1 could also be used as a lead-in to this activity.

Procedure
- Divide the class into groups of four and explain that each of these groups is made up of two pairs. One person in each pair is going to do the negotiation (the negotiator) while the other makes notes about what his or her partner says during the negotiation (the scribe). The group can decide who plays which role.
- Give out the information sheet to each learner and allow time for them to read 'Your company'. Give them time for questions. If there is enough time, let them come up with a company profile on their own or in a brainstorming session.
- Give one of the negotiators in each group the role card of the senior marketing manager and the other one the role card of the head of R&D. Each of the negotiators then works with his/her scribe and discusses 'Your role' on the information sheet (making sure that the other negotiator does not hear what they decide). They fill out this information before the negotiation begins. The information can be based on the actual personality of the learner or can be invented. As they may come from a totally different area of business, the learners should think carefully about what type of person they are before beginning the negotiation.
- The negotiation begins. Each scribe makes notes about what was said by 'their' negotiator.
- When the negotiation has finished (or when the teacher gives a signal to stop), the scribes read their notes aloud to each other in the form of a second negotiation. This enables the negotiators to listen to their own words and notice if what they meant to say came across in the way it was intended. (This is why it is important that the scribe helps to decide on the profile of the negotiator.)
- Finally, the groups compare the differences in the negotiation. Was one negotiator more successful than the other? Were they exactly the same? Did the profiles have any elements of truth in them? Did the personalities of the negotiators make a difference to the outcome? Was consensus achieved? Why or why not?

Follow-up
If negotiating is important to the learners, the exercise could be repeated in a later lesson. In this case, the scribes and negotiators should change roles and the class can go through the activity again.

One-to-one
The teacher and learner can take one role each to do the negotiation and then discuss the results at the end. The teacher can work on language as well as negotiating techniques.

Note
This activity allows some learners to listen carefully and make notes (a realistic situation in the working world) and others to find out if they were clear in what they wanted to express. They also have the chance to 'observe themselves' and can reflect on what happened in the negotiating process. This can be looked at as a pure language activity (making notes, paraphrasing, etc.) or as negotiating training in which learners have a period of self-reflection.

Vocabulary
core business key products or services of a company
diagnostic serving to identify a particular problem
healthcare sector businesses dealing with medical needs and supplies
shareholder value keeping the value of a corporation as high as possible in the interests of the shareholders

Information

Your company

Your company is in the healthcare sector and one of its core businesses is the development of highly sophisticated diagnostic machines. The advantage of these machines is that they can be used by doctors in their surgeries or even by patients at home. The machines are linked through external software to databases and diagnostic centres in hospitals so that the results can be processed immediately. This field is growing at the moment and there is a lot of competition among the companies working in it.

Problems and challenges

Your company has an excellent reputation, but other companies are beginning to increase their market shares. All of your products already include software, but the software packages linking the machines have to be sold separately. If quality of both machines and software is not maintained, there could be a reduction in sales, leading to lower profits. The pressure to maintain and preferably increase market share is very high.

Current situation

Your company employs over 50,000 people worldwide and has always been known for highly innovative and reliable products. However, due to the recession in the global economy, your board of directors has made it clear that market share as well as shareholder value are high priorities and must be accomplished.

Your role

Think about the role (either the senior marketing manager or the head of R&D) you will be playing and create your character. Talk to your scribe and decide how to answer the following questions about your new role after looking at the role card.

Do you prefer to be more formal or informal in clothing, speech, etc.?

Do you prefer to use first names, last names or titles?

Is small talk important to you?

You have never met your negotiating partner before.

What do you think this person has heard about you?

Are you an experienced negotiator or is this one of your first negotiations?

Is there anything else about you which is important to consider?

(age, gender, education, nationality, etc.)

Roles

Senior marketing manager

Background information

- You studied business and when you finished six years ago, you joined this company.
- You were recently transferred to your current location from the headquarters in another country so you don't know everyone at this new location yet.

Your responsibilities

- You have to sell the IT support systems for diagnostic machines made by your company.
- You have to meet sales targets set by the board of directors.

Your problems and challenges

- Many of your competitors give their support packages away free of charge but you are not allowed to do that.
- Your support package is becoming outdated and it is time for the next generation of software.
- R&D had been working on a new package but stopped a few months ago when the head of R&D decided that the entire staff of four people was needed to work on a new state-of-the art diagnostic machine due to come out in three years.
- You feel strongly that at least 75% of the R&D team should continue to work on the software package.

Important information for you

- You understand that development of a new product is also vital to the success of the company but you are afraid that the new diagnostic machine will be very difficult to sell because there won't be any customers left to buy it. They will have all switched to your competitors because your software programs will not be up-to-date. You have to make R&D understand this problem.

Plan of action

- Set up a meeting with the head of R&D. Try to convince him or her that you need at least three people to create the next generation of software.

Head of R&D

Background information

- You studied electrical engineering and began working at this company a number of years ago.

Your responsibilities

- You have to constantly try to develop the most up-to-date equipment on the market.

Your problems and challenges

- You have a small team of four engineers to work with and they are already stretched to their limits.
- Your department had been working on a project to update current software but you heard about a competitor's plans to come out with a better product and you decided it was more important to develop a new and improved diagnostic machine.
- You cancelled the new software project so that your department could spend its time working on the new equipment.
- You would like to be able to hire at least two more engineers as the group is putting in 10 to 15 hours of overtime per week on average.

Important information for you

- You feel that the company's survival depends on these highly developed products because the field is so competitive. The sales and marketing teams don't really understand the problems faced by R&D and complain quite often about how difficult it is to sell the products. You think that if you can develop the best product on the market, they will certainly have an easier time selling it.

Plan of action

- Agree to a meeting with the marketing manager. Try to convince him or her that new product development has to take priority over updating older systems.

11.1 Presentations

Key phrases

Type of activity
Gap-fill

Time
20 minutes, with discussion

Level
Intermediate–Upper intermediate / B1–B2

Language focus
Presentations phrases

Group formation
Pairs or small groups

Preparation
Copy and cut up a set of gapped sentences cards and prepositions cards for each group.

Lead-in
Discuss how often the learners have to give a presentation or think they may have to in future. Talk about what is involved and what makes a good presenter.

Write the following headings on the board: Greetings and introduction, Preview, Body of the presentation, Review, Closing, and give examples. (These can be from the cards or other general examples of presentation language.) Then add the more specific categories of: Ordering, Moving on, Giving good news, Giving bad news, Using visuals. Explain that these additional categories can fit into the more general ones given above. Ask learners to brainstorm phrases that could fit into these categories. Write them under the appropriate heading.

Procedure
- Divide the class into pairs or small groups and give out the cards.
- Get the learners to work out which preposition is missing in each of the gapped sentences and see if the preposition they think completes the sentence is on one of the cards. Point out that most prepositions appear on more than one card. When they are sure that they have the correct preposition for a particular gap, the learners should write the preposition in the gap and put the relevant preposition card to one side. It will help the learners if they do the ones they are sure of first.
- When they have filled in as many gaps as possible, check answers and then get the learners to organize their sentences cards into the categories given above. As the specific categories are included within a more general category, some cards will belong to more than one category, for example, 'Bad news' and 'Body'.
- Discuss the answers with the learners (see Introduction).

Follow-up
The learners write down the sentences, with their categories, that they feel are useful for them.

The learners try to think of other phrases which fit into the various categories.

One-to-one
The teacher brainstorms phrases with the learner. Then the learner matches the cards and discusses them with the teacher. The learner and the teacher then discuss which category the sentences fit into.

Note
It is important to get learners to say these phrases aloud and to make them automatic. They need to be able to think on their feet in a presentation, and by repeating phrases aloud in an activity, it is possible to learn them in both a visual and an auditory way.

Explain the difference between internal and external presentations. Tell the learners that normally bad news would only come in an informative internal presentation and not in most external ones.

Vocabulary
to bring someone up-to-date to inform someone of the latest developments
chart a visualization (normally of figures or amounts) in the form of a diagram
figures numbers
to hand out/round to give written information to a group of people
premises a place where business is conducted, usually including buildings and grounds
product line a group of products which have something in common with each other
product range the products produced or sold by a company
to recap to review or repeat what one has said
sales results the actual amount which has been sold
sales targets the specific amount which is expected to be sold

Gapped sentences

1
I would like to welcome you all ________ our new premises this morning.

2
For those who don't know me, my name is Fiona Henry and I am ________ Dowell, Inc.

3
I'm going to start ________ by showing you the latest figures.

4
Today you are going to hear ________ our sales targets.

5
The first part of my presentation will deal ________ new marketing strategies.

6
After that I am going to go ________ / ________ some new procedures.

7
Leaving this topic ________ the moment, I would like you to turn your attention ________ these sales results.

8
Now I would like to move ________ to the next topic.

9
This brings me ________ my next point.

10
If you would just take a look ________ this chart, you'll see what I mean.

11
I am going to hand ________ / ________ some information for you to look at.

12
We are extremely optimistic ________ our new product range.

13
We are very proud ________ the new product line.

14
We are sure that we are ________ the way to recovery.

15
In the last two years, our sales figures have fallen ________ five per cent.

16
It is clear to all of us that certain steps have to be taken to keep more problems ________ arising.

17
I would like to recap ________ what I have just said.

18
I would just like to point ________ the main issues we covered today.

19
And to sum up, we have complete confidence ________ the new products.

20
________ conclusion, I feel it is necessary to mention that we will have to rethink some of our sales strategies.

21
I hope this presentation has brought you up-to-date ________ the latest developments.

22
Thank you all ________ taking the time to come here today.

Prepositions

to	from	off	about
with	over / through	for	to
on	to	at	out / round
about	of	on	by
from	on	out	in
in	with	for	

Key

Greetings and introduction (G&I)
Preview (P)
Body (B)
Review (R)
Closing (C)
Ordering (O)
Moving on (MO)
Visuals (V)
Good News (GN)
Bad News (BN)

1 I would like to welcome you all **to** our new premises this morning. **(G&I)**	2 For those who don't know me, my name is Fiona Henry and I am **from** Dowell, Inc. **(G&I)**	3 I'm going to start **off** by showing you the latest figures. **(P)**	4 Today you are going to hear **about** our sales targets. **(P)**
5 The first part of my presentation will deal **with** new marketing strategies. **(P, O)**	6 After that I am going to go **over / through** some new procedures. **(P, O)**	7 Leaving this topic **for** the moment, I would like you to turn your attention **to** these sales results. **(B, MO)**	8 Now I would like to move **on** to the next topic. **(B, MO)**
9 This brings me **to** my next point. **(B, MO)**	10 If you would just take a look **at** this chart, you'll see what I mean. **(B, V)**	11 I am going to hand **out / round** some information for you to look at. **(B, V)**	12 We are extremely optimistic **about** our new product range. **(B, GN)**
13 We are very proud **of** the new product line. **(B, GN)**	14 We are sure that we are **on** the way to recovery. **(B, GN)**	15 In the last two years, our sales figures have fallen **by** five per cent. **(B, BN)**	16 It is clear to all of us that certain steps have to be taken to keep more problems **from** arising. **(B, BN)**
17 I would like to recap **on** what I have just said. **(R)**	18 I would just like to point **out** the main issues we covered today. **(R)**	19 And to sum up, we have complete confidence **in** the new products. **(R, C)**	20 **In** conclusion, I feel it is necessary to mention that we will have to rethink some of our sales strategies. **(R, C)**
21 I hope this presentation has brought you up-to-date **with** the latest developments. **(C)**	22 Thank you all **for** taking the time to come here today. **(C)**		

Giving a presentation

Type of activity

Presenting and giving feedback

Time

15–20 minutes to prepare presentations

15–20 minutes per presentation, with feedback

Depending on the size of the class, this can be done over several lessons or the preparation part could be given as homework

Level

Upper intermediate–Advanced / B2–C1

Language focus

Language of presentations

Linking words

Group formation

Whole class

Preparation

Copy the sheet on preparing a presentation, one for each learner.

Copy the topic cards for the class and cut them up, enough for two or three for each learner.

Copy the sheet on feedback, one for each learner.

Lead-in

Discuss how often the learners have to give a presentation or think they may have to in the future. Talk about what is involved and what makes a good presenter.

Activity 11.1 could also be used as a lead-in to this activity.

Procedure

- Give the worksheet on preparation to each learner in the class.
- Let the learners choose a topic card. Make enough sets to allow the learners to have a good choice of topics; let them choose another card if they really don't want to use the topic they first chose. Alternatively, the sheet with the topic cards could be copied onto an OHT so that the learners could choose from the entire set. Point out that each topic card contains useful vocabulary, but they don't have to use any of it if they don't want to.
- Write these linking words on the board:
  For the preview: *first of all, secondly, then, next, after this*
  For the body: *at this point, after all, basically, in general, according to, is/was caused by, as a result of, due to, in order to*
  For the review and conclusion: *finally, in conclusion, to sum up*
- Give the learners time to make notes about their presentation on the presentation preparation worksheet. Make it clear that the audience will be the other learners and that this is a chance to practise presentation techniques in a safe atmosphere.
- Give out the feedback sheets. Tell the learners that you only want to hear positive feedback. (When people hear negative feedback, they only know what *not* to do, but not what they should do. They often replace one negative habit with another. Giving them positive feedback helps them strengthen the areas which work well and leads to overall improvement.)
- Hold the presentations – set a time limit of 5–10 minutes per person.
- Learners watch the presentations, make notes and give feedback to the presenters when they are over.
- The presenters are then asked for feedback on their own presentations. This brings in the element of self-reflection, and they can think specifically of the things they were happy about and what they would like to improve.

One-to-one

The learner can choose a topic from the cards or decide on a topic for himself or herself and prepare a presentation for the teacher. The teacher then fills in the feedback sheet and discusses it with the learner. The learner should also be given time for self-reflection.

Note

The topics for the presentations include specific business areas as well as more general ones. The idea behind this is to find something that everyone can talk about and to give the learners the opportunity to talk about general areas of interest in front of others. This can be used with experienced business people or with learners who have not yet worked in the business environment.

Preparation

Greetings and introduction • Greet your audience and tell them who you are and where you are from.
Preview • Begin your presentation and list the main points you plan to cover.
Body of the presentation • Give the details. • Use linking sentences to move from one point to another. • Structure your presentation. Put specific categories within a main category. • Consider how to move on, give good and bad news, and use visuals, as appropriate.
Review • Sum up and go over your main points again. • List the main points and remind your audience what you have told them.
Closing • Thank your audience for coming and for their attention.

Topics

The global economy recession, recovery, rise, fall, boom, slump, reach a low/high, forecast, trade debt	**Cross-cultural relationships** diversity, knowledge, tolerance, acceptance, customs, traditions, festivals, ethics, prejudices, stereotypes, communication styles	**Sales update** movement, increase, decrease, outside factors, figures, improvement, confidence, challenge, targets, market share	**Advertising** print media, TV and radio commercials, strategies, point-of-sale, promotions, market research, campaign, markets, branding
Office management time-keeping, breaks, training, procedures, paperwork, emails, efficiency, time management, organization	**Presentations** visual aids, Powerpoint, overhead projector (OHP), transparencies, slides, graphs, charts, notes, audience, structure, data projector	**Meetings** set up, arrange, agenda, hidden agenda, taking the minutes, problem-solving, time limitations, consensus, motions, seconding, AOB, put to the vote	**Small talk** greetings, socializing, restaurants, formal, informal, first names, titles, introductions, communicating, dining, arrangements
Information technology communication, the internet, networks, provider, browser, operating system, peripherals, state-of-the-art, USB stick, CD ROM burner, install, crash, data	**Telephone etiquette** answer the phone, transfer a call, put through, spell, articulate, clear speaking voice, enquiries, put on hold, get back to someone	**Customer relations** complaints, apologies, refund, discount, credit note, hotline, technical support, manual, guarantee	**Import and export** duty, domestic, international, forwarding agent, means of transport, documentation, consignment, shipping costs, letter of credit
Budgets forecast, estimate, expenditure, income, revenue, targets, figures, update, analysis, chartered accountant	**Business travel** airline, flight connections, lounge, departure, arrival, itinerary, laptop, reimbursement, expense account, credit card	**Banking** current account, savings account, loan, credit rating, interest, mortgage, fees and charges, standing order, direct deposit, direct debit	**Work/Life balance** fast track, job-sharing, hot-desking, telecommuting, responsibilities, time off, time in lieu, holidays, part-time, full-time, stress, time management

Feedback

Specific things I liked about the presentation (posture, gestures, voice, register, structure, pace, clarity, interest, contact with the audience)
Details I noticed about the presentation
Phrases I noted down
Ideas I got which I would like to try out myself

The culture game

Type of activity
Board game

Time
20–30 minutes

Level
Intermediate–Upper intermediate / B1–B2

Language focus
Vocabulary related to customs and cultures

Group formation
Groups of three to five

Preparation
Copy the board game, one copy for each group. It is best to enlarge the board game and copy it onto A3 paper, and, if possible, laminate it.

Copy and cut up the cards, one set for each group.

Have a dice and counter for each group.

Lead-in
Ask learners how often they do business with people from other countries. Find out which countries they deal with and ask if anyone has a story to tell about an encounter with someone from another country.

Procedure
- Give the board game and one set of cards to each group. The players take turns to move around the board by throwing the dice and moving the same number of squares as shown on the dice.
- Each of the squares either has information which must be discussed, an instruction to move forwards or backwards or miss a turn, or a question card. The questions on the squares are about the specific country the player who landed on the square comes from. There are no right or wrong answers; they simply give that player the chance to say something about his or her culture.
- The questions on the question cards are asked by the player to the right of the person who lands on the square. These are general and business-specific questions about different countries and include answers so that the learners are not dependent on the teacher. If the player answers correctly, he or she moves forward one square.
- The winner is the player who reaches the Finish square first.

One-to-one
This game can be played with the teacher and one learner. Alternatively, the question cards can be discussed without the rest of the board game.

Note
The learners aren't necessarily expected to know the answers to the questions on the question cards. The answers are given to provide the learners with information as well as discussion points.

Vocabulary
chatter insignificant conversation
densely populated a large number of people living in a small area of land
ladle a large spoon used for removing liquids from a container
literacy being able to read and write
venue a place where a specific event takes place

Question cards

Which country has the largest population? China. There are about 1.2 billion people living there.	*Which is the largest country in the world?* Russia. It comprises 17 million km^2.	*Which city is the most densely populated in the world?* Hong Kong.
What language is spoken by most people in the world? Mandarin (Chinese). It is spoken by about one billion people.	*Is English the official or major language in more or fewer than 30 countries?* More. It is the official or major language in 46 countries.	*What is the largest religion in the world?* Islam. It has over 1.1 billion followers.
In which country do people traditionally eat 12 grapes at midnight on New Year's Eve? Spain. They put one grape in their mouths for each chime of the clock.	*In which country does the bather stand outside a type of bath called a mandri?* Indonesia. The bather dips a ladle in the water and pours it over him or herself.	*How should you accept a Japanese person's business card?* You should take it with both hands (and study it with interest).
Which country in Europe has the highest percentage of women working outside the home? Denmark. It is one of the most progressive countries when it comes to equality between men and women.	*Is it polite or impolite to arrive punctually at a social event in Argentina?* Impolite. You should arrive 30–60 minutes late.	*Which hand do Arabs accept gifts with?* Their right hand.
In Belgium, should you shake hands with everyone (including children)? Yes.	*Do business people generally come on time to appointments in Brazil?* No. They can be 15–30 minutes late.	*What is the largest French-speaking city outside of France?* Montreal, Canada.
Is the literacy rate high or low in Chile? It is very high, about 95%. Chileans are very proud of this.	*If you are applauded after being introduced to a group in China, what should you do?* You should applaud back.	*Does government play a major or minor role in business in France?* A major one. Local representatives are very important for doing business.
In a German company do people leave their doors open or closed? They are generally closed and it is necessary to knock before entering.	*What is the day of rest for Muslims?* Friday.	*Is business conducted on the golf course in Ireland?* Yes. This is a major venue for business deals and discussions.
On what date do Polish people have their Christmas meal and exchange gifts? December 24th.	*Is silence acceptable in Japan in a business meeting?* Yes. This is considered non-verbal communication and better than chatter.	*Are drinks in Malaysia offered and accepted with one hand or two hands?* With two hands.
Is it all right to refuse an offer of something to drink in Mexico? No. It is considered rude.	*Does food play a major role in hospitality in the Netherlands?* No. Do not expect to be served a meal unless it is mentioned in the invitation.	*Which unusual activity may take place at a business dinner in the Philippines?* Singing. You will be expected to join in.
Which colour is considered lucky in China? Red.	*What day is considered unlucky in Spain?* Tuesday the 13th.	*Do Italians drink cappuccino at breakfast, lunch or dinner?* Breakfast. It is considered ignorant to ask for a cappuccino with lunch or dinner.
How many states are there in the USA? Fifty.	*Are contracts in Taiwan written or verbal?* They are verbal.	*How many countries make up the United Kingdom?* Four. England, Scotland, Wales and Northern Ireland. Refer to them collectively as the UK or separately by nationality.

Board game

Talk about your country

- Start and Finish
- Describe a custom.
- What is a traditional meal?
- Talk about a national holiday.
- Question card
- Miss a turn.
- What do people do in their leisure time?
- Is there a traditional drink?
- The other players each advance one square.
- Question card
- How do people greet each other?
- Advance one square.
- How do people dress for business?
- Question card
- What is the major religion?
- The other players go back one square.
- Is there a traditional gift to bring to a host or hostess?

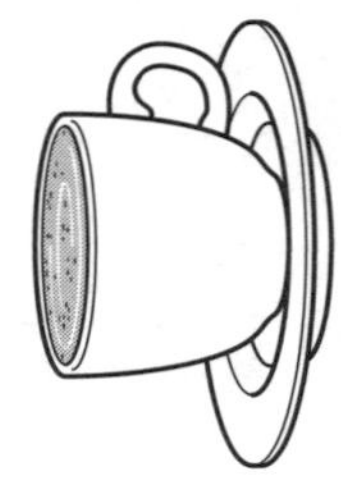
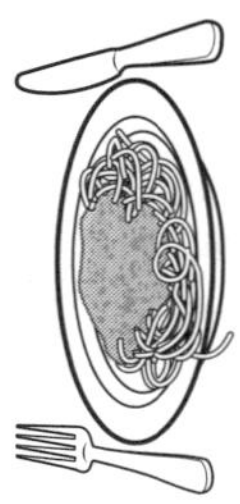

UK or US?

Type of activity
Information gap

Time
20 minutes

Level
Intermediate / B1

Language focus
British vs American terms

Group formation
Groups of four

Preparation
Copy sheets A, B, C and D, one sheet per learner.

Lead-in
Have a discussion about the differences in language used by native English speakers in different parts of the world. Learners can contribute their experiences to this discussion. Explain that it is often necessary to understand the different phrases used by British and American native speakers in particular, and that depending on where they learned English, non-natives may also have a preference for either British or American English.

Give some examples such as *lift / elevator, roundabout / traffic circle, petrol station / gas station* (British English first in each pair).

Elicit the questions *What is the British/American term for …?* and *What is the definition of …?* and write them on the board.

Procedure
- Divide the class into groups of four, divided into two pairs (A and B, C and D).
- Give each person a copy of the grid and instruct him or her to fill out the grid by speaking to his or her partner but without looking at his or her partner's sheet. Advise the learners asking for information to give the two pieces of information they have, e.g. *What is the definition of time in lieu? It's American name is comp time.* When the partners have got all the information they can (some is missing), they then make new pairs (A and C, B and D).
- Discuss the answers with the learners (see Introduction).

Follow-up
This activity can be followed up with a writing activity. Tell the learners that they are either two British business people or two American business people (one in finance and one in human resources) sharing a taxi from an airport to a meeting in town. Each group of four should invent the dialogue which takes place while the two business people are travelling together. Encourage groups to use other phrases and vocabulary that they know as well as words from the grid.

When the groups finish, they give their dialogues to a group who had the opposite native speakers and they replace the British words with American ones, or the American words with British ones.

Alternatively, a group could write a short text using the expressions and another group then replaces the words using either the British or the American equivalents. This should encourage learners to use the vocabulary actively and quickly recognize which of these expressions is used by one group or the other.

One-to-one
The learner and the teacher fill in the gaps together by asking and answering questions.

Note
This activity can also be done by moving around the classroom and trying to fill in the grids by finding those who have the information a particular learner is missing.

The word *billboard* is found in British English but *hoarding* is not common in the United States.

Definitions A

	British	Definition	American
1	*current account*	an active account at a bank which allows the customer to deposit and withdraw money (usually in the form of cheques)	
2	*time in lieu*		*comp time (compensatory time)*
3	*Inland Revenue*	the government institution responsible for taxation	
4	*Directory Enquiries*		*Directory Assistance*
5		portable, wireless telephone	*cellphone*
6	*personal assistant (PA)*	person appointed to assist a manager or director often working more independently than a secretary	
7	*cashpoint / cash machine*	a machine where you use a card and PIN number to withdraw money from a bank account	
8	*upmarket / downmarket*	goods of high or low quality and price	
9	*unit trust*	a portfolio of securities managed by a central administration for the customer	
10		qualified accountant who is legally allowed to deal with audits, taxation and balance sheets	*certified public accountant (CPA)*
11	*CV (curriculum vitae)*		*resumé*
12	*file*	a folder with rings to store office documents	
13		a device made of rubber to delete writing in pencil	*eraser*
14	*hoarding*	a large sign used for advertising	
15		money given to a worker or employee as compensation for having to leave a company	*severance pay*
16	*building society*		*savings and loan association*
17		a small book with a separate space for each day for writing arrangements, notes, etc.	*appointment book*
18	*annual leave*	time off from work which is part of an employee's benefits	

Definitions B

	British	Definition	American
1	*current account*	an active account at a bank which allows the customer to deposit and withdraw money (often in the form of cheques)	
2		time off for extra time worked	*comp time (compensatory time)*
3		the government institution responsible for taxation	*Internal Revenue Service (IRS)*
4	*Directory Enquiries*		*Directory Assistance*
5	*mobile phone*	portable, wireless telephone	
6	*personal assistant (PA)*		*executive assistant*
7		a machine where you use a card and PIN number to withdraw money from a bank account	*ATM (automatic teller machine)*
8		goods of high or low quality and price	*upscale / downscale*
9	*unit trust*		*mutual fund*
10	*chartered accountant*	qualified accountant who is legally allowed to deal with audits, taxation and balance sheets	
11		a written record of education and work experience	*resumé*
12	*file*	a folder with rings to store office documents	
13	*rubber*	a device made of rubber to delete writing in pencil	
14		a large sign used for advertising	*billboard*
15	*redundancy pay*		*severance pay*
16	*building society*	a financial institution specializing in loans for purchasing and building homes	
17		a small book with a separate space for each day for writing arrangements, notes, etc.	*appointment book*
18	*annual leave*	time off from work which is part of an employee's benefits	

Definitions C

	British	Definition	American
1	*current account*		*checking account*
2		time off for extra time worked	*comp time (compensatory time)*
3		the government institution responsible for taxation	*Internal Revenue Service (IRS)*
4	*Directory Enquiries*	a service which supplies telephone numbers to callers	
5	*mobile phone*		*cellphone*
6		person appointed to assist a manager or director often working more independently than a secretary	*executive assistant*
7	*cashpoint / cash machine*	a machine where you use a card and PIN number to withdraw money from a bank account	
8	*upmarket / downmarket*		*upscale / downscale*
9		a portfolio of securities managed by a central administration for the customer	*mutual fund*
10	*chartered accountant*	qualified accountant who is legally allowed to deal with audits, taxation and balance sheets	
11		a written record of education and work experience	*resumé*
12		a folder with rings to store office documents	*binder*
13		a device made of rubber to delete writing in pencil	*eraser*
14	*hoarding*	a large sign used for advertising	
15	*redundancy pay*		*severance pay*
16	*building society*	a financial institution specializing in loans for purchasing and building homes	
17	*diary*		*appointment book*
18	*annual leave*		*paid vacation*

Definitions D

	British	Definition	American
1	*current account*		*checking account*
2	*time in lieu*		*comp time (compensatory time)*
3	*Inland Revenue*	the government institution responsible for taxation	
4	*Directory Enquiries*	a service which supplies telephone numbers to callers	
5		portable, wireless telephone	*cellphone*
6		person appointed to assist a manager or director and often working more independently than a secretary	*executive assistant*
7	*cashpoint / cash machine*		*ATM (automatic teller machine)*
8	*upmarket / downmarket*	goods of high or low quality and price	
9		a portfolio of securities managed by a central administration for the customer	*mutual fund*
10		qualified accountant who is legally allowed to deal with audits, taxation and balance sheets	*certified public accountant (CPA)*
11	*CV (curriculum vitae)*	a written record of education and work experience	
12		a folder with rings to store office documents	*binder*
13	*rubber*	a device made of rubber to delete writing in pencil	
14	*hoarding*		*billboard*
15	*redundancy pay*	money given to a worker or employee as compensation for having to leave a company	
16		a financial institution specializing in loans for purchasing and building homes	*savings and loan association*
17	*diary*	a small book with a separate space for each day for writing arrangements, notes. etc.	
18		time off from work which is part of an employee's benefits	*paid vacation*

Key

	British	Definition	American
1	*current account*	an active account at a bank which allows the customer to deposit and withdraw money (usually in the form of cheques)	*checking account*
2	*time in lieu*	time off for extra time worked	*comp time (compensatory time)*
3	*Inland Revenue*	the government institution responsible for taxation	*Internal Revenue Service (IRS)*
4	*Directory Enquiries*	a service which supplies telephone numbers to callers	*Directory Assistance*
5	*mobile phone*	portable, wireless telephone	*cellphone*
6	*personal assistant (PA)*	person appointed to assist a manager or director often working more independently than a secretary	*executive assistant*
7	*cashpoint / cash machine*	a machine where you use a card and PIN number to withdraw money from a bank account	*ATM (automatic teller machine)*
8	*upmarket / downmarket*	goods of high or low quality and price	*upscale / downscale*
9	*unit trust*	a portfolio of securities managed by a central administration for the customer	*mutual fund*
10	*chartered accountant*	qualified accountant who is legally allowed to deal with audits, taxation and balance sheets	*certified public accountant (CPA)*
11	*CV (curriculum vitae)*	a written record of education and work experience	*resumé*
12	*file*	a folder with rings to store office documents	*binder*
13	*rubber*	a device made of rubber to delete writing in pencil	*eraser*
14	*hoarding*	a large sign used for advertising	*billboard*
15	*redundancy pay*	money given to a worker or employee as compensation for having to leave a company	*severance pay*
16	*building society*	a financial institution specializing in loans for purchasing and building homes	*savings and loan association*
17	*diary*	a small book with a separate space for each day for writing arrangements, notes, etc.	*appointment book*
18	*annual leave*	time off from work which is part of an employee's benefits	*paid vacation*

British/American triangle

Type of activity
Matching

Time
15 minutes

Level
Intermediate / B1

Language focus
British vs American terms

Group formation
Groups of three

Preparation
Copy and cut up the vocabulary triangle grid, sheets A, B and C, for each group of learners.

Lead-in
Brainstorm common British and American English terms, e.g. *lift / elevator* and explain that it is often necessary to understand the different phrases used by British and American native speakers.

Activity 13.1 could also be used as a lead-in to this activity.

Procedure
- Divide the class into three groups. In large classes, these groups can be subdivided into smaller groups.
- Give each learner in a group one of the sheets of the vocabulary triangle (A, B or C).
- Tell them that the American English terms are in the left-hand column and the British equivalents are in the right-hand column. The equivalents to the words on their sheet match with ones on the sheets which the other learners have. They must work together to find the correct equivalents.
- Learner A begins by reading the word in the top left-hand corner. B and C look for the equivalent on the right-hand side of the page and when someone has found it, he or she reads it aloud. Then he or she reads the word directly opposite (on the same line) to the other two learners, who look for the equivalent word and read the word opposite, and so on. The last word to be read is the word in the top right-hand corner of sheet A.

One-to-one
The learner can work with one of the sheets, while the teacher uses the other two. A strong learner could have two of the sheets while the teacher has one.

Note
The vocabulary triangle can be used either as a review of vocabulary which has already been taught or as a way of introducing new vocabulary. In the latter case, it would be done before Activity 13.1, which contains all the equivalents used in this activity.

British/American triangle

A

certified public accountant (CPA)	*diary*
ATM (automatic teller machine)	*CV (curriculum vitae)*
upscale / downscale	*unit trust*
comp time (compensatory time)	*Directory Enquiries*
Internal Revenue Service (IRS)	*mobile phone*
paid vacation	*redundancy pay*

B

eraser	*hoarding*
savings and loan association	*annual leave*
checking account	*Inland Revenue*
binder	*chartered accountant*
appointment book	*personal assistant (PA)*
resumé	*upmarket / downmarket*

C

cellphone	*cashpoint / cash machine*
severance pay	*file*
executive assistant	*current account*
mutual fund	*rubber*
Directory Assistance	*building society*
billboard	*time in lieu*